THE KENTONS

William Dean Howells

1st WORLD
LIBRARY
Literary Society

The Kentons

William Dean Howells

© 1st World Library, 2006
PO Box 2211
Fairfield, IA 52556
www.1stworldlibrary.com
First Edition

LCCN: 2006935366

Softcover ISBN: 1-4218-2511-2
Hardcover ISBN: 1-4218-2411-6
eBook ISBN: 1-4218-2611-9

Purchase *"The Kentons"*
as a traditional bound book at:
www.1stWorldLibrary.com/purchase.asp?ISBN=1-4218-2511-2

1st World Library is a literary, educational organization
dedicated to:

- Creating a free internet library of downloadable ebooks

- Hosting writing competitions and offering book
publishing scholarships.

Interested in more 1st World Library books?
contact: literacy@1stworldlibrary.com
Check us out at: www.1stworldlibrary.com

1st World Library Literary Society

Giving Back to the World

"If you want to work on the core problem, it's early school literacy."

- James Barksdale, former CEO of Netscape

"No skill is more crucial to the future of a child, or to a democratic and prosperous society, than literacy."

- Los Angeles Times

Literacy... means far more than learning how to read and write... The aim is to transmit... knowledge and promote social participation."

- UNESCO

"Literacy is not a luxury, it is a right and a responsibility. If our world is to meet the challenges of the twenty-first century we must harness the energy and creativity of all our citizens."

- President Bill Clinton

"Parents should be encouraged to read to their children, and teachers should be equipped with all available techniques for teaching literacy, so the varying needs and capacities of individual kids can be taken into account."

- Hugh Mackay

I

The Kentons were not rich, but they were certainly richer than the average in the pleasant county town of the Middle West, where they had spent nearly their whole married life. As their circumstances had grown easier, they had mellowed more and more in the keeping of their comfortable home, until they hated to leave it even for the short outings, which their children made them take, to Niagara or the Upper Lakes in the hot weather. They believed that they could not be so well anywhere as in the great square brick house which still kept its four acres about it, in the heart of the growing town, where the trees they had planted with their own hands topped it on three aides, and a spacious garden opened southward behind it to the summer wind. Kenton had his library, where he transacted by day such law business as he had retained in his own hands; but at night he liked to go to his wife's room and sit with her there. They left the parlors and piazzas to their girls, where they could hear them laughing with the young fellows who came to make the morning calls, long since disused in the centres of fashion, or the evening calls, scarcely more authorized by the great world. She sewed, and he read his paper in her satisfactory silence, or they played checkers together. She did not like him to win, and when she found herself unable to bear the prospect of defeat, she refused to let him make the move that threatened the safety of her men. Sometimes he laughed at her, and sometimes he scolded, but they were very good comrades, as elderly married people are apt to be. They had long ago quarrelled out their serious differences, which mostly arose from such differences of temperament as had first drawn them together; they criticised each other to their children from time to time, but they atoned for this defection by complaining of the children to each other, and they united in giving way to them on all points concerning their happiness, not to say their pleasure.

They had both been teachers in their youth before he went into the war, and they had not married until he had settled himself in the practice of the law after he left the army. He was then a man of thirty, and five years older than she; five children were born to them, but the second son died when he was yet a babe in his mother's arms, and there was an interval of six years between the first boy and the first girl. Their eldest son was already married, and settled next them in a house which was brick, like their own, but not square, and had grounds so much less ample that he got most of his vegetables from their garden. He had grown naturally into a share of his father's law practice, and he had taken it all over when Renton was elected to the bench. He made a show of giving it back after the judge retired, but by that time Kenton was well on in the fifties. The practice itself had changed, and had become mainly the legal business of a large corporation. In this form it was distasteful to him; he kept the affairs of some of his old clients in his hands, but he gave much of his time, which he saved his self-respect by calling his leisure, to a history of his regiment in-the war.

In his later life he had reverted to many of the preoccupations of his youth, and he believed that Tuskingum enjoyed the best climate, on the whole, in the union; that its people of mingled Virginian, Pennsylvanian, and Connecticut origin, with little recent admixture of foreign strains, were of the purest American stock, and spoke the best English in the world; they enjoyed obviously the greatest sum of happiness, and had incontestibly the lowest death rate and divorce rate in the State. The growth of the place was normal and healthy; it had increased only to five thousand during the time he had known it, which was almost an ideal figure for a county-town. There was a higher average of intelligence than in any other place of

William Dean Howells

its size, and a wider and evener diffusion of prosperity. Its record in the civil war was less brilliant, perhaps, than that of some other localities, but it was fully up to the general Ohio level, which was the high-water mark of the national achievement in the greatest war of the greatest people under the sun. It, was Kenton's pride and glory that he had been a part of the finest army known in history. He believed that the men who made history ought to write it, and in his first Commemoration-Day oration he urged his companions in arms to set down everything they could remember of their soldiering, and to save the letters they had written home, so that they might each contribute to a collective autobiography of the regiment. It was only in this way, he held, that the intensely personal character of the struggle could be recorded. He had felt his way to the fact that every battle is essentially episodical, very campaign a sum of fortuities; and it was not strange that he should suppose, with his want of perspective, that this universal fact was purely national and American. His zeal made him the repository of a vast mass of material which he could not have refused to keep for the soldiers who brought it to him, more or less in a humorous indulgence of his whim. But he even offered to receive it, and in a community where everything took the complexion of a joke, he came to be affectionately regarded as a crank on that point; the shabbily aging veterans, whom he pursued to their workbenches and cornfields, for, the documents of the regimental history, liked to ask the colonel if he had brought his gun. They, always give him the title with which he had been breveted at the close of the war; but he was known to the younger, generation of his fellow-citizens as the judge. His wife called him Mr. Kenton in the presence of strangers, and sometimes to himself, but to his children she called him Poppa, as they did.

The steady-going eldest son, who had succeeded to his father's affairs without giving him the sense of dispossession, loyally accepted the popular belief that he would never be the man his father was. He joined with his mother in a respect for Kenton's theory of the regimental history which was none the less sincere because it was unconsciously a little sceptical of the outcome; and the eldest daughter was of their party. The youngest said frankly that she had no use for any history, but she said the same of nearly everything which had not directly or indirectly to do with dancing. In this regulation she had use for parties and picnics, for buggy-rides and sleigh-rides, for calls from young men and visits to and from other girls, for concerts, for plays, for circuses and church sociables, for everything but lectures; and she devoted herself to her pleasures without the shadow of chaperonage, which was, indeed, a thing still unheard of in Tuskingum.

In the expansion which no one else ventured, or, perhaps, wished to set bounds to, she came under the criticism of her younger brother, who, upon the rare occasions when he deigned to mingle in the family affairs, drew their mother's notice to his sister's excesses in carrying-on, and required some action that should keep her from bringing the name, of Kenton to disgrace. From being himself a boy of very slovenly and lawless life he had suddenly, at the age of fourteen, caught himself up from the street, reformed his dress and conduct, and confined himself in his large room at the top of the house, where, on the pursuits to which he gave his spare time, the friends who frequented his society, and the literature which nourished his darkling spirit, might fitly have been written Mystery. The sister whom he reprobated was only two years his elder, but since that difference in a girl accounts for a great deal, it apparently authorized her to take him more lightly than he was able to take himself. She said that he was in love, and she achieved an importance with him through his speechless rage and scorn which none of the rest of his family enjoyed. With his father and mother he had a bearing of repressed superiority which a strenuous conscience kept from unmasking itself in open contempt when they failed to make his sister promise to behave herself. Sometimes he had lapses from his dignified gloom with his mother, when, for no reason that could be given, he fell from his habitual majesty to the tender dependence of a little boy, just as his voice broke from its nascent base to its earlier treble at moments when he least expected or wished such a thing to happen. His stately but vague ideal of himself was supported by a stature beyond his years, but this rendered it the more difficult for him to bear the humiliation of his sudden collapses, and made him at other times the easier prey of Lottie's ridicule. He got on best, or at least most evenly, with his eldest sister. She took him seriously, perhaps because she took all life so; and she was able to interpret him to his father when his intolerable dignity forbade a common understanding between them. When he got so far beyond his depth that he did not know what he meant himself, as sometimes happened, she gently found him a safe footing nearer shore.

Kenton's theory was that he did not distinguish among his children. He said that he did not suppose they were the best children in the world, but they suited him; and he would not have known how to change them for the better. He saw no harm in the behavior of Lottie when it most shocked her brother; he liked her to have a good time; but it flattered his nerves to have Ellen about him. Lottie was a great deal more accomplished, he allowed that; she could play and sing, and she had social gifts far beyond her sister; but he easily proved to his wife that Nelly knew ten times as much.

Nelly read a great deal; she kept up with all the magazines, and knew all the books in his library. He believed that she was a fine German scholar, and in fact she had taken up that language after leaving school, when, if she had been better advised than she could have been in Tuskingum, she would have kept on with her French. She started the first book club in the place; and she helped her father do the intellectual honors of the house to the Eastern lecturers, who always stayed with the judge when they came to Tuskingum. She was faithfully present at the moments, which her sister shunned in derision, when her father explained to them respectively his theory of regimental history, and would just, as he said, show them a few of the documents he had collected. He made Ellen show them; she knew where to put her hand on the most characteristic and illustrative; and Lottie offered to bet what one dared that Ellen would marry some of those lecturers yet;

she was literary enough.

She boasted that she was not literary herself, and had no use for any one who was; and it could not have been her culture that drew the most cultivated young man in Tuskingum to her. Ellen was really more beautiful; Lottie was merely very pretty; but she had charm for them, and Ellen, who had their honor and friendship, had no charm for them. No one seemed drawn to her as they were drawn to her sister till a man came who was not one of the most cultivated in Tuskingum; and then it was doubtful whether she was not first drawn to him. She was too transparent to hide her feeling from her father and mother, who saw with even more grief than shame that she could not hide it from the man himself, whom they thought so unworthy of it.

He had suddenly arrived in Tuskingum from one of the villages of the county, where he had been teaching school, and had found something to do as reporter on the Tuskingum 'Intelligencer', which he was instinctively characterizing with the spirit of the new journalism, and was pushing as hardily forward on the lines of personality as if he had dropped down to it from the height of a New York or Chicago Sunday edition. The judge said, with something less than his habitual honesty, that he did not mind his being a reporter, but he minded his being light and shallow; he minded his being flippant and mocking; he minded his bringing his cigarettes and banjo into the house at his second visit. He did not mind his push; the fellow had his way to make and he had to push; but he did mind his being all push; and his having come out of the country with as little simplicity as if he had passed his whole life in the city. He had no modesty, and he had no reverence; he had no reverence for Ellen herself, and the poor girl seemed to like him for that.

He was all the more offensive to the judge because he was himself to blame for their acquaintance, which began when one day the fellow had called after him in the street, and then followed down the shady sidewalk beside him to his hour, wanting to know what this was he had heard about his history, and pleading for more light upon his plan in it. At the gate he made a flourish of opening and shutting it for the judge, and walking up the path to his door he kept his hand on the judge's shoulder most offensively; but in spite of this Kenton had the weakness to ask him in, and to call Ellen to get him the most illustrative documents of the history.

The interview that resulted in the 'Intelligencer' was the least evil that came of this error. Kenton was amazed, and then consoled, and then afflicted that Ellen was not disgusted with it; and in his conferences with his wife he fumed and fretted at his own culpable folly, and tried to get back of the time he had committed it, in that illusion which people have with trouble that it could somehow be got rid of if it could fairly be got back of; till the time came when his wife could no longer share his unrest in this futile endeavor.

She said, one night when they had talked late and long, "That can't be helped now; and the question is what are we going to do to stop it."

The judge evaded the point in saying, "The devil of it is that all the nice fellows are afraid of her; they respect her too much, and the very thing which ought to disgust her with this chap is what gives him his power over her. I don't know what we are going to do, but we must break it off, somehow."

"We might take her with us somewhere," Mrs. Kenton suggested.

"Run away from the fellow? I think I see myself! No, we have got to stay and face the thing right here. But I won't have him about the house any more, understand that. He's not to be let in, and Ellen mustn't see him; you tell her I said so. Or no! I will speak to her myself." His wife said that he was welcome to do that; but he did not quite do it. He certainly spoke to his daughter about her, lover, and he satisfied himself that there was yet nothing explicit between them. But she was so much less frank and open with him than she had always been before that he was wounded as well as baffled by her reserve. He could not get her to own that she really cared for the fellow; but man as he was, and old man as he was, he could not help perceiving that she lived in a fond dream of him.

He went from her to her mother. "If he was only one-half the man she thinks he is!" - he ended his report in a hopeless sigh.

"You want to give in to her!" his wife pitilessly interpreted. "Well, perhaps that would be the best thing, after all."

"No, no, it wouldn't, Sarah; it would be the easiest for both of us, I admit, but it would be the worst thing for her. We've got to let it run along for a while yet. If we give him rope enough he may hang himself; there's that chance. We can't go away, and we can't shut her up, and we can't turn him out of the house. We must trust her to find him out for herself."

"She'll never do that," said the mother. "Lottie says Ellen thinks he's just perfect. He cheers her up, and takes her out of herself. We've always acted with her as if we thought she was different from other girls, and he behaves to her as if she was just like all of them, just as silly, and just as weak, and it pleases her, and flatters her; she likes it."

"Oh, Lord!" groaned the father. "I suppose she does."

This was bad enough; it was a blow to his pride in Ellen; but there was something that hurt him still worse. When the fellow had made sure of her, he apparently felt himself so safe in her fondness that he did not urge his suit with her. His content with her tacit acceptance gave the bitterness of shame to the promise Kenton and his wife had made each other never to cross any of their children in love. They were ready now to keep that promise for Ellen, if he asked it of them, rather than answer for her lifelong disappointment, if they denied him. But, whatever he meant finally to do, he did not ask it; he used his footing in their house chiefly as a basis for flirtations beyond it. He began to share his devotions to Ellen with her girl friends, and not with her girl friends alone. It did not come to scandal, but it certainly came to gossip about him and a silly young wife; and Kenton heard of it with a torment of doubt whether Ellen knew of it, and what she would do; he would wait for her to do herself whatever was to be done. He was never certain how much she had heard of the gossip when she came to her mother, and said with the gentle eagerness she had, "Didn't poppa talk once of going South this winter?"

"He talked of going to New York," the mother answered, with a throb of hope.

"Well," the girl returned, patiently, and Mrs. Kenton read in her passivity an eagerness to be gone from sorrow that she would not suffer to be seen, and interpreted her to her father in such wise that he could not hesitate.

II

If such a thing could be mercifully ordered, the order of this event had certainly been merciful; but it was a cruel wrench that tore Kenton from the home where he had struck such deep root. When he actually came to leave the place his going had a ghastly unreality, which was heightened by his sense of the common reluctance. No one wanted to go, so far as he could make out, not even Ellen herself, when he tried to make her say she wished it. Lottie was in open revolt, and animated her young men to a share in the insurrection. Her older brother was kindly and helpfully acquiescent, but he was so far from advising the move that Kenton had regularly to convince himself that Richard approved it, by making him say that it was only for the winter and that it was the best way of helping Ellen get rid of that fellow. All this did not enable Kenton to meet the problems of his younger son, who required him to tell what he was to do with his dog and his pigeons, and to declare at once how he was to dispose of the cocoons he had amassed so as not to endanger the future of the moths and butterflies involved in them. The boy was so fertile in difficulties and so importunate for their solution, that he had to be crushed into silence by his father, who ached in a helpless sympathy with his reluctance.

Kenton came heavily upon the courage of his wife, who was urging forward their departure with so much energy that he obscurely accused her of being the cause of it, and could only be convinced of her innocence when she offered to give the whole thing up if he said so. When he would not say so, she

William Dean Howells

carried the affair through to the bitter end, and she did not spare him some, pangs which she perhaps need not have shared with him. But people are seldom man and wife for half their lives without wishing to impart their sufferings as well as their pleasures to each other; and Mrs. Kenton, if she was no worse, was no better than other wives in pressing to her husband's lips the cup that was not altogether sweet to her own. She went about the house the night before closing it, to see that everything was in a state to be left, and then she came to Kenton in his library, where he had been burning some papers and getting others ready to give in charge to his son, and sat down by his cold hearth with him, and wrung his soul with the tale of the last things she had been doing. When she had made him bear it all, she began to turn the bright side of the affair to him. She praised the sense and strength of Ellen, in the course the girl had taken with herself, and asked him if he, really thought they could have done less for her than they were doing. She reminded him that they were not running away from the fellow, as she had once thought they must, but Ellen was renouncing him, and putting him out of her sight till she could put him out of her mind. She did not pretend that the girl had done this yet; but it was everything that she wished to do it, and saw that it was best. Then she kissed him on his gray head, and left him alone to the first ecstasy of his homesickness.

It was better when they once got to New York, and were settled in an apartment of an old-fashioned down-town hotel. They thought themselves very cramped in it, and they were but little easier when they found that the apartments over and under them were apparently thought spacious for families of twice their numbers. It was the very quietest place in the whole city, but Kenton was used to the stillness of Tuskingum, where, since people no longer kept hens, the nights were stiller than in the country itself; and for a week he slept badly. Otherwise, as soon as they got used to living in six rooms instead of seventeen, they were really very comfortable.

He could see that his wife was glad of the release from

housekeeping, and she was growing gayer and seemed to be growing younger in the inspiration of the great, good-natured town. They had first come to New York on their wedding journey, but since that visit she had always let him go alone on his business errands to the East; these had grown less and less frequent, and he had not seen New York for ten or twelve years. He could have waited as much longer, but he liked her pleasure in the place, and with the homesickness always lurking at his heart he went about with her to the amusements which she frequented, as she said, to help Ellen take her mind off herself. At the play and the opera he sat thinking of the silent, lonely house at Tuakingum, dark among its leafless maples, and the life that was no more in it than if they had all died out of it; and he could not keep down a certain resentment, senseless and cruel, as if the poor girl were somehow to blame for their exile. When he betrayed this feeling to his wife, as he sometimes must, she scolded him for it, and then offered, if he really thought anything like that, to go back to Tuskingum at once; and it ended in his having to own himself wrong, and humbly promise that he never would let the child dream how he felt, unless he really wished to kill her. He was obliged to carry his self-punishment so far as to take Lottie very sharply to task when she broke out in hot rebellion, and declared that it was all Ellen's fault; she was not afraid of killing her sister; and though she did not say it to her, she said it of her, that anybody else could have got rid of that fellow without turning the whole family out of house and home.

Lottie, in fact, was not having a bit good time in New York, which she did not find equal in any way to Tuskingum for fun. She hated the dull propriety of the hotel, where nobody got acquainted, and every one was as afraid as death of every one else; and in her desolation she was thrown back upon the society of her brother Boyne. They became friends in their common dislike of New York; and pending some chance of bringing each other under condemnation they lamented their banishment from Tuskingum together. But even Boyne contrived to make the heavy time pass more lightly than she in

William Dean Howells

the lessons he had with a tutor, and the studies of the city which he carried on. When the skating was not good in Central Park he spent most of his afternoons and evenings at the vaudeville theatres. None of the dime museums escaped his research, and he conversed with freaks and monsters of all sorts upon terms of friendly confidence. He reported their different theories of themselves to his family with the same simple-hearted interest that he criticised the song and dance artists of the vaudeville theatres. He became an innocent but by no means uncritical connoisseur of their attractions, and he surprised with the constancy and variety of his experience in them a gentleman who sat next him one night. Boyne thought him a person of cultivation, and consulted him upon the opinion he had formed that there was not so much harm in such places as people said. The gentleman distinguished in saying that he thought you would not find more harm in them, if you did not bring it with you, than you would in the legitimate theatres; and in the hope of further wisdom from him, Boyne followed him out of the theatre and helped him on with his overcoat. The gentleman walked home to his hotel with him, and professed a pleasure in his acquaintance which he said he trusted they might sometime renew.

All at once the Kentons began to be acquainted in the hotel, as often happens with people after they have long ridden up and down in the elevator together in bonds of apparently perpetual strangeness. From one friendly family their acquaintance spread to others until they were, almost without knowing it, suddenly and simultaneously on smiling and then on speaking terms with the people of every permanent table in the dining-room. Lottie and Boyne burst the chains of the unnatural kindness which bound them, and resumed their old relations of reciprocal censure. He found a fellow of his own age in the apartment below, who had the same country traditions and was engaged in a like inspection of the city; and she discovered two girls on another floor, who said they received on Saturdays and wanted her to receive with them. They made a tea for her, and asked some real New Yorkers; and such a round of pleasant little events began for her that Boyne was forced to call his mother's attention to the way Charlotte was going on with the young men whom she met and frankly asked to call upon her without knowing anything about them; you could not do that in New York, he said.

But by this time New York had gone to Mrs. Kenton's head, too, and she was less fitted to deal with Lottie than at home. Whether she had succeeded or not in helping Ellen take her mind off herself, she had certainly freed her own from introspection in a dream of things which had seemed impossible before. She was in that moment of a woman's life which has a certain pathos for the intelligent witness, when, having reared her children and outgrown the more incessant cares of her motherhood, she sometimes reverts to her girlish impulses and ideals, and confronts the remaining opportunities of life with a joyful hope unknown to our heavier and sullener sex in its later years. It is this peculiar power of rejuvenescence which perhaps makes so many women outlive their husbands, who at the same age regard this world as an accomplished fact. Mrs. Kenton had kept up their reading long after Kenton found himself too busy or too tired for it; and when he came from his office at night and fell asleep over the book she wished him to hear, she continued it herself, and told him about it. When Ellen began to show the same taste, they read together, and the mother was not jealous when the father betrayed that he was much prouder of his daughter's culture than his wife's. She had her own misgivings that she was not so modern as Ellen, and she accepted her judgment in the case of some authors whom she did not like so well.

She now went about not only to all the places where she could make Ellen's amusement serve as an excuse, but to others when she could not coax or compel the melancholy girl. She was as constant at matinees of one kind as Boyne at another sort; she went to the exhibitions of pictures, and got herself up in schools of painting; she frequented galleries, public and private, and got asked to studio teas; she went to meetings and conferences of aesthetic interest, and she paid an easy way to parlor lectures expressive of the vague but profound ferment in women's souls; from these her presence in intellectual clubs was a simple and natural transition. She met and talked with interesting people, and now and then she got introduced to literary people. Once, in a book-store, she stood next to a gentleman leaning over the same counter, whom a salesman addressed by the name of a popular author, and she remained staring at him breathless till he left the place. When she bragged of the prodigious experience at home, her husband defied her to say how it differed from meeting the lecturers who had been their guests in Tuskingum, and she answered that none of them compared with this author; and, besides, a lion in his own haunts was very different from a lion going round the country on exhibition. Kenton thought that was pretty good, and owned that she had got him there.

He laughed at her, to the children, but all the same she believed that she was living in an atmosphere of culture, and with every breath she was sensible of an intellectual expansion. She found herself in the enjoyment of so wide and varied a sympathy with interests hitherto strange to her experience that she could not easily make people believe she had never been to Europe. Nearly every one she met had been several times, and took it for granted that she knew the Continent as well as they themselves.

She denied it with increasing shame; she tried to make Kenton understand how she felt, and she might have gone further if she had not seen how homesick he was for Tuskingum. She did her best to coax him and scold him into a share of the pleasure they were all beginning to have in New York. She made him own that Ellen herself was beginning to be gayer; she convinced him that his business was not suffering in his absence and that he was the better from the complete rest he was having. She defied him, to say, then, what was the matter with him, and she bitterly reproached herself, in the event, for not having known that it was not homesickness alone that was the trouble. When he was not going about with her, or doing something to amuse the children, he went upon long, lonely walks, and came home silent and fagged. He had given up smoking, and he did not care to sit about in the office of the hotel where other old fellows passed the time over their papers and cigars, in the heat of the glowing grates. They looked too much like himself, with their air of unrecognized consequence, and of personal loss in an alien environment. He knew from their dress and bearing that they were country people, and it wounded him in a tender place to realize that they had each left behind him in his own town an authority and a respect which they could not enjoy in New York. Nobody called them judge, or general, or doctor, or squire; nobody cared who they were, or what they thought; Kenton did not care himself; but when he missed one of them he envied him, for then he knew that he had gone back to the soft, warm keeping of his own neighborhood, and resumed the intelligent regard of a community he had grown up with. There were men in New York whom Kenton had met in former years, and whom he had sometimes fancied looking up; but he did not let them know he was in town, and then he was hurt that they ignored him. He kept away from places where he was likely to meet them; he thought that it must have come to them that he was spending the winter in New York, and as bitterly as his nature would suffer he resented the indifference of the Ohio Society to the presence of an Ohio man of his local distinction. He had not the habit of clubs, and when one of the pleasant younger fellows whom he met in the hotel offered to put him up at one, he shrank from the courtesy shyly and almost dryly. He had outlived the period of active curiosity, and he did not explore the city as he world once have done. He had no resorts out of the hotel, except the basements of the secondhand book-dealers. He haunted these, and picked up copies of war histories and biographies, which, as fast as he read them, he sent off to his son at Tuskingum, and had him put them away with the documents for the life of his regiment. His wife could see, with compassion if not sympathy, that he was fondly strengthening by these means the ties that bound him to his home, and she silently proposed to go back to it with him whenever he should say the word.

He had a mechanical fidelity, however, to their agreement that they should stay till spring, and he made no sign of going, as the winter wore away to its end, except to write out to Tuskingum minute instructions for getting the garden ready. He varied his visits to the book-stalls by conferences with seedsmen at their stores; and his wife could see that he had as keen a satisfaction in despatching a rare find from one as from the other.

She forbore to make him realize that the situation had not changed, and that they would be taking their daughter back to the trouble the girl herself had wished to escape. She was trusting, with no definite hope, for some chance of making him feel this, while Kenton was waiting with a kind of passionate patience for the term of his exile, when he came in one day in April from one of his long walks, and said he had been up to the Park to see the blackbirds. But he complained of being tired, and he lay down on his bed. He did not get up for dinner, and then it was six weeks before he left his room.

He could not remember that he had ever been sick so long before, and he was so awed by his suffering, which was severe but not serious, that when his doctor said he thought a voyage to Europe would be good for him he submitted too meekly for Mrs. Kenton. Her heart smote her for her guilty joy in his sentence, and she punished herself by asking if it would not do him more good to get back to the comfort and quiet of their own house. She went to the length of saying that she believed his attack had been brought on more by homesickness than anything else. But the doctor agreed rather with her wish than her word, and held out that his melancholy was not the cause but the effect of his disorder. Then she took courage and began getting ready to go. She did not flag even in the dark hours when Kenton got back his courage with his returning strength, and scoffed at the notion of Europe, and insisted that as soon as they were in Tuskingum he should be all right again.

She felt the ingratitude, not to say the perfidy, of his behavior, and she fortified herself indignantly against it; but it was not her constant purpose, or the doctor's inflexible opinion, that prevailed with Kenton at last a letter came one day for Ellen which she showed to her mother, and which her mother, with her distress obscurely relieved by a sense of its powerful instrumentality, brought to the girl's father. It was from that fellow, as they always called him, and it asked of the girl a hearing upon a certain point in which, it had just come to his knowledge, she had misjudged him. He made no claim upon her, and only urged his wish to right himself with her because she was the one person in the whole world, after his mother, for whose good opinion he cared. With some tawdriness of sentiment, the letter was well worded; it was professedly written for the sole purpose of knowing whether, when she came back to Tuskingum, she would see him, and let him prove to her that he was not wholly unworthy of the kindness she had shown him when he was without other friends.

"What does she say?" the judge demanded.

"What do you suppose?" his wife retorted. "She thinks she ought to see him."

"Very well, then. We will go to Europe."

"Not on my account!" Mrs. Kenton consciously protested.

"No; not on your account, or mine, either. On Nelly's account. Where is she? I want to talk with her."

"And I want to talk with you. She's out, with Lottie; and when she comes back I will tell her what you say. But I want to know what you think, first."

III

It was some time before they arrived at a common agreement as to what Kenton thought, and when they reached it they decided that they must leave the matter altogether to Ellen, as they had done before. They would never force her to anything, and if, after all that her mother could say, she still wished to see the fellow, they would not deny her.

When it came to this, Ellen was a long time silent, so long a time that her mother was beginning restively to doubt whether she was going to speak at all. Then she drew a long, silent breath. "I suppose I ought to despise myself, momma, for caring for him, when he's never really said that he cared for me."

"No, no," her mother faltered.

"But I do, I do!" she gave way piteously. "I can't help it! He doesn't say so, even now."

"No, he doesn't." It hurt her mother to own the fact that alone gave her hope.

The girl was a long time silent again before she asked, "Has poppa got the tickets?"

"Why, he wouldn't, Ellen, child, till he knew how you felt," her mother tenderly reproached her.

"He'd better not wait!" The tears ran silently down Ellen's cheeks, and her lips twitched a little between these words and the next; she spoke as if it were still of her father, but her mother understood. "If he ever does say so, don't you speak a word to me, momma; and don't you let poppa."

"No; indeed I won't," her mother promised. "Have we ever interfered, Ellen? Have we ever tried to control you?"

"He WOULD have said so, if he hadn't seen that everybody was against him." The mother bore without reply the ingratitude and injustice that she knew were from the child's pain and not from her will. "Where is his letter? Give me his letter!" She nervously twitched it from her mother's hand and ran it into her pocket. She turned away to go and put off her hat, which she still wore from coming in with Lottie; but she stopped and looked over her shoulder at her mother. "I'm going to answer it, and I don't want you ever to ask me what I've said. Will you?"

"No, I won't, Nelly."

"Well, then!"

The next night she went with Boyne and Lottie to the apartment overhead to spend their last evening with the young people there, who were going into the country the next day. She came back without the others, who wished to stay a little longer, as she said, with a look of gay excitement in her eyes, which her mother knew was not happiness. Mrs. Kenton had an impulse to sweep into her lap the lithograph plans of the steamer, and the passage ticket which lay open on the table before herself and her husband. But it was too late to hide them from Ellen. She saw them, and caught up the ticket, and read it, and flung it down again. "Oh, I didn't think you would do it!" she burst out; and she ran away to her room, where they could hear her sobbing, as they sat haggardly facing each other.

"Well, that settles it," said Benton at last, with a hard gulp.

"Oh, I suppose so," his wife assented.

On his part, now, he had a genuine regret for her disappointment from the sad safety of the trouble that would keep them at home; and on her part she could be glad of it if any sort of comfort could come out of it to him.

"Till she says go," he added, "we've got to stay."

"Oh yes," his wife responded. "The worst of it is, we can't even go back to Tuskingum." He looked up suddenly at her, and she saw that he had not thought of this. She made "Tchk!" in sheer amaze at him.

"We won't cross that river till we come to it," he said, sullenly, but half-ashamed. The next morning the situation had not changed overnight, as they somehow both crazily hoped it might, and at breakfast, which they had at a table grown more remote from others with the thinning out of the winter guests of the hotel, the father and mother sat down alone in silence which was scarcely broken till Lottie and Boyne joined them.

"Where's Ellen?" the boy demanded.

"She's having her breakfast in her room," Mrs. Kenton answered.

"She says she don't want to eat anything," Lottie reported. "She made the man take it away again."

The gloom deepened in the faces of the father and mother, but neither spoke, and Boyne resumed the word again in a tone of philosophic speculation. "I don't see how I'm going to get along, with those European breakfasts. They say you can't get anything but cold meat or eggs; and generally they don't expect to give you anything but bread and butter with your coffee. I don't think that's the way to start the day, do you, poppa?"

Kenton seemed not to have heard, for he went on silently eating, and the mother, who had not been appealed to, merely looked distractedly across the table at her children.

"Mr. Plumpton says he's coming down to see us off," said Lottie, smoothing her napkin in her lap. "Do you know the time of day when the boat sails, momma?"

"Yes," her brother broke in, "and if I had been momma I'd have boxed your ears for the way you went on with him. You fairly teased him to come. The way Lottie goes on with men is a shame, momma."

"What time does the boat sail, momma!" Lottie blandly persisted. "I promised to let Mr. Plumpton know."

"Yes, so as to get a chance to write to him," said Boyne. "I guess when he sees your spelling!"

"Momma! Do wake up! What time does our steamer sail?"

A light of consciousness came into Mrs. Renton's eyes at last, and she sighed gently. "We're not going, Lottie."

"Not going! Why, but we've got the tickets, and I've told -"

"Your father has decided not to go, for the present. We may go later in the summer, or perhaps in the fall."

Boyne looked at his father's troubled face, and said nothing, but Lottie was not stayed from the expression of her feelings by any ill-timed consideration for what her father's might be. "I just know," she fired, "it's something to do with that nasty Bittridge. He's been a bitter dose to this family! As soon as I saw Ellen have a letter I was sure it was from him; and she ought to be ashamed. If I had played the simpleton with such a fellow I guess you wouldn't have let me keep you from going to Europe very much. What is she going to do now? Marry him? Or doesn't he want her to?"

"Lottie!" said her mother, and her father glanced up at her with a face that silenced her.

"When you've been half as good a girl as Ellen has been, in this whole matter," he said, darkly, "it will be time for you to complain of the way you've been treated."

"Oh yes, I know you like Ellen the best," said the girl, defiantly.

"Don't say such a thing, Lottie!" said her mother. "Your father loves all his children alike, and I won't have you talking so to him. Ellen has had a great deal to bear, and she has behaved beautifully. If we are not going to Europe it is because we have decided that it is best not to go, and I wish to hear nothing more from you about it."

"Oh yes! And a nice position it leaves me in, when I've been taking good-bye of everybody! Well, I hope to goodness you won't say anything about it till the Plumptons get away. I couldn't have the face to meet them if you did."

"It won't be necessary to say anything; or you can say that we've merely postponed our sailing. People are always doing that."

"It's not to be a postponement," said Kenton, so sternly that no one ventured to dispute him, the children because they were afraid of him, and their mother because she was suffering for him.

At the steamship office, however, the authorities represented that it was now so near the date of his sailing that they could not allow him to relinquish his passages except at his own risk. They would try to sell his ticket for him, but they could not take it back, and they could not promise to sell it. There was reason in what they said, but if there had been none, they had the four hundred dollars which Kenton had paid for his five berths and they had at least the advantage of him in the argument by that means. He put the ticket back in his pocket-book without attempting to answer them, and deferred his decision till he could advise with his wife, who, after he left the breakfast-table upon his errand to the steamship office, had abandoned her children to their own devices, and gone to scold Ellen for not eating.

She had not the heart to scold her when she found the girl lying face downward in the pillow, with her thin arms thrown up through the coils and heaps of her loose-flung hair. She was so alight that her figure scarcely defined itself under the bedclothes; the dark hair, and the white, outstretched arms seemed all there was of her. She did not stir, but her mother knew she was not sleeping. "Ellen," she said, gently, "you needn't be troubled about our going to Europe. Your father has gone down to the steamship office to give back his ticket."

The girl flashed her face round with nervous quickness. "Gone to give back his ticket!"

"Yes, we decided it last night. He's never really wanted to go, and -"

"But I don't wish poppa to give up his ticket!" said Ellen. "He must get it again. I shall die if I stay here, momma. We have got to go. Can't you understand that?"

Mrs. Kenton did not know what to answer. She had a strong superficial desire to shake her daughter as a naughty child which has vexed its mother, but under this was a stir stronger pity for her as a woman, which easily, prevailed. "Why, but, Ellen dear! We thought from what you said last night -"

"But couldn't you SEE," the girl reproached her, and she began to cry, and turned her face into the pillow again and lay sobbing.

"Well," said her mother, after she had given her a little time, "you needn't be troubled. Your father can easily get the ticket again; he can telephone down for it. Nothing has been done yet. But didn't you really want to stay, then?"

"It isn't whether I want to stay or not," Ellen spoke into her pillow. "You know that. You know that I have got to go. You know that if I saw him - Oh, why do you make me talk?"

"Yes, I understand, child." Then, in the imperious necessity of blaming some one, Mrs. Kenton added: "You know how it is with your father. He is always so precipitate; and when he heard what you said, last night, it cut him to the heart. He felt as if he were dragging you away, and this morning he could hardly wait to get through his breakfast before he rushed down to the steamship office. But now it's all right again, and if you want to go, we'll go, and your father will only be too glad."

"I don't want father to go against his will. You said he never wanted to go to Europe." The girl had turned her face upon her mother again; and fixed her with her tearful, accusing eyes.

"The doctors say he ought to go. He needs the change, and I think we should all be the better far getting away."

"I shall not," said Ellen. "But if I don't -"

"Yes," said her mother, soothingly.

"You know that nothing has changed. He hasn't changed and I haven't. If he was bad, he's as bad as ever, and I'm just as silly. Oh, it's like a drunkard! I suppose they know it's killing them, but they can't give it up! Don't you think it's very strange, momma? I don't see why I should be so. It seems as if I had no character at all, and I despise myself so! Do you believe I shall ever get over it? Sometimes I think the best thing for me would be to go into an asylum."

"Oh yes, dear; you'll get over it, and forget it all. As soon as you see others - other scenes - and get interested -"

"And you don't you don't think I'd better let him come, and -"

"Ellen!"

Ellen began to sob again, and toss her head upon the pillow. "What shall I do? What shall I do?" she wailed. "He hasn't ever done anything bad to me, and if I can overlook his - his flirting - with that horrid thing, I don't know what the rest of you have got to say. And he says he can explain everything. Why shouldn't I give him the chance, momma? I do think it is acting very cruel not to let him even say a word."

"You can see him if you wish, Ellen," said her mother, gravely. "Your father and I have always said that. And perhaps it would be the best thing, after all."

"Oh, you say that because you think that if I did see him, I should be so disgusted with him that I'd never want to speak to him again. But what if I shouldn't?"

"Then we should wish you to do whatever you thought was for your happiness, Ellen. We can't believe it would be for your good; but if it would be for your happiness, we are willing. Or, if you don't think it's for your happiness, but only for his, and you wish to do it, still we shall be willing, and you know that as far as your father and I are concerned, there will never be a word of reproach - not a whisper."

"Lottie would despise me; and what would Richard say?"

"Richard would never say anything to wound you, dear, and if you don't despise yourself, you needn't mind Lottie."

"But I should, momma; that's the worst of it! I should despise myself, and he would despise me too. No, if I see him, I am going to do it because I am selfish and wicked, and wish to have my own way, no matter who is harmed by it, or - anything; and I'm not going to have it put on any other ground. I could see him," she said, as if to herself, "just once more - only once more - and then if I didn't believe in him, I could start right off to Europe."

Her mother made no answer to this, and Ellen lay awhile apparently forgetful of her presence, inwardly dramatizing a passionate scene of dismissal between herself and her false lover. She roused herself from the reverie with a long sigh, and her mother said, "Won't you have some breakfast, now; Ellen?"

"Yes; and I will get up. You needn't be troubled any more about me, momma. I will write to him not to come, and poppa must go back and get his ticket again."

"Not unless you are doing this of your own free will, child. I can't have you feeling that we are putting any pressure upon you."

"You're not. I'm doing it of my own will. If it isn't my free will, that isn't your fault. I wonder whose fault it is? Mine, or what made me so silly and weak?"

"You are not silly and weak," said her mother, fondly, and she bent over the girl and would have kissed her, but Ellen averted her face with a piteous "Don't!" and Mrs. Kenton went out and ordered her breakfast brought back.

She did not go in to make her eat it, as she would have done in the beginning of the girl's trouble; they had all learned how much better she was for being left to fight her battles with herself singlehanded. Mrs. Kenton waited in the parlor till her husband same in, looking gloomy and tired. He put his hat down and sank into a chair without speaking. "Well?" she said.

"We have got to lose the price of the ticket, if we give it back. I thought I had better talk with you first," said Kenton, and he explained the situation.

"Then you had better simply have it put off till the next steamer. I have been talking with Ellen, and she doesn't want to stay. She wants to go." His wife took advantage of Kenton's mute amaze (in the nervous vagaries even of the women nearest him a man learns nothing from experience) to put her own interpretation on the case, which, as it was creditable to the girl's sense and principle, he found acceptable if not imaginable. "And if you will take my advice," she ended, "you will go quietly back to the steamship office and exchange your ticket for the next steamer, or the one after that, if you can't get good rooms, and give Ellen time to get over this before she leaves. It will be much better for her to conquer herself than to run away, for that would always give her a feeling of shame, and if she decides before she goes, it will strengthen her pride and self-respect, and there will be less danger - when we come back."

"Do you think he's going to keep after her!"

"How can I tell? He will if he thinks it's to his interest, or he can make anybody miserable by it."

Kenton said nothing to this, but after a while he suggested, rather timorously, as if it were something he could not expect her to approve, and was himself half ashamed of, "I believe if I do put it off, I'll run out to Tuskingum before we sail, and look after a little matter of business that I don't think Dick can attend to so well."

His wife knew why he wanted to go, and in her own mind she had already decided that if he should ever propose to go, she should not gainsay him. She had, in fact, been rather surprised that he had not proposed it before this, and now she assented, without taxing him with his real motive, and bringing him to open disgrace before her. She even went further in saying: "Very well, then you had better go. I can get on very well here, and I think it will leave Ellen freer to act for herself if you are away. And there are some things in the house that I want, and that Richard would be sure to send his wife to get if I asked him, and I won't have her rummaging around in my closets. I suppose you will want to go into the house?"

"I suppose so," said Renton, who had not let a day pass, since he left his house, without spending half his homesick time in it. His wife suffered his affected indifference to go without exposure, and trumped up a commission for him, which would take him intimately into the house.

IV

The piety of his son Richard had maintained the place at Tuskingum in perfect order outwardly, and Kenton's heart ached with tender pain as he passed up the neatly kept walk from the gate, between the blooming ranks of syringas and snowballs, to his door, and witnessed the faithful care that Richard's hired man had bestowed upon every detail. The grass between the banks of roses and rhododendrons had been as scrupulously lawn-mowered and as sedulously garden-hosed as if Kenton himself had been there to look after its welfare, or had tended the shrubbery as he used to do in earlier days with his own hand. The oaks which he had planted shook out their glossy green in the morning gale, and in the tulip-trees, which had snowed their petals on the ground in wide circles defined by the reach of their branches, he heard the squirrels barking; a red-bird from the woody depths behind the house mocked the cat-birds in the quince-trees. The June rose was red along the trellis of the veranda, where Lottie ought to be sitting to receive the morning calls of the young men who were sometimes quite as early as Kenton's present visit in their devotions, and the sound of Ellen's piano, played fitfully and absently in her fashion, ought to be coming out irrespective of the hour. It seemed to him that his wife must open the door as his steps and his son's made themselves heard on the walk between the box borders in their upper orchard, and he faltered a little.

"Look here, father," said his son, detecting his hesitation. "Why don't you let Mary come in with you, and help you find

William Dean Howells

those things?"

"No, no," said Kenton, sinking into one of the wooden seats that flanked the door-way. "I promised your mother that I would get them myself. You know women don't like to have other women going through their houses."

"Yes, but Mary!" his son urged.

"Ah! It's just Mary, with her perfect housekeeping, that your mother wouldn't like to have see the way she left things," said Kenton, and he smiled at the notion of any one being housekeeper enough to find a flaw in his wife's. "My, but this is pleasant!" he added. He took off his hat and let the breeze play through the lank, thin hair which was still black on his fine, high forehead. He was a very handsome old man, with a delicate aquiline profile, of the perfect Roman type which is perhaps oftener found in America than ever it was in Rome. "You've kept it very nice, Dick," he said, with a generalizing wave of his hat.

"Well, I couldn't tell whether you would be coming back or not, and I thought I had better be ready for you."

"I wish we were," said the old man, "and we shall be, in the fall, or the latter part of the summer. But it's better now that we should go - on Ellen's account."

"Oh, you'll enjoy it," his son evaded him.

"You haven't seen anything of him lately?" Kenton suggested.

"He wasn't likely to let me see anything of him," returned the son.

"No," said the father. "Well!" He rose to put the key into the door, and his son stepped down from the little porch to the brick walk.

"Mary will have dinner early, father; and when you've got through here, you'd better come over and lie down a while beforehand."

Kenton had been dropped at eight o'clock from a sleeper on the Great Three, and had refused breakfast at his son's house, upon the plea that the porter had given him a Southern cantaloupe and a cup of coffee on the train, and he was no longer hungry.

"All right," he said. "I won't be longer than I can help." He had got the door open and was going to close it again.

His son laughed. "Better not shut it, father. It will let the fresh air in."

"Oh, all right," said the old man.

The son lingered about, giving some orders to the hired man in the vegetable garden, for an excuse, in the hope that his father might change his mind and ask him to come into the house with him; he felt it so forlorn for him to be going through those lifeless rooms alone. When he looked round, and saw his father holding the door ajar, as if impatiently waiting for him to be gone, he laughed and waved his hand to him. "All right, father? I'm going now." But though he treated the matter so lightly with his father, he said grimly to his wife, as he passed her on their own porch, on his way to his once, "I don't like to think of father being driven out of house and home this way."

"Neither do I, Dick. But it can't be helped, can it?"

"I think I could help it, if I got my hands on that fellow once."

"No, you couldn't, Dick. It's not he that's doing it. It's Ellen; you know that well enough; and you've just got to stand it."

"Yes, I suppose so," said Richard Kenton.

William Dean Howells

"Of course, my heart aches for your poor old father, but so it would if Ellen had some kind of awful sickness. It is a kind of sickness, and you can't fight it any more than if she really was sick."

"No," said the husband, dejectedly. "You just slip over there, after a while, Mary, if father's gone too long, will you? I don't like to have him there alone."

"'Deed and 'deed I won't, Dick. He wouldn't like it at all, my spying round. Nothing can happen to him, and I believe your mother's just made an excuse to send him after something, so that he can be in there alone, and realize that the house isn't home any more. It will be easier for him to go to Europe when he finds that out. I believe in my heart that was her idea in not wanting me to find the things for him, and I'm not going to meddle myself."

With the fatuity of a man in such things, and with the fatuity of age regarding all the things of the past, Kenton had thought in his homesickness of his house as he used to be in it, and had never been able to picture it without the family life. As he now walked through the empty rooms, and up and down the stairs, his pulse beat low as if in the presence of death. Everything was as they had left it, when they went out of the house, and it appeared to Kenton that nothing had been touched there since, though when he afterwards reported to his wife that there was not a speck of dust anywhere she knew that Mary had been going through the house, in their absence, not once only, but often, and she felt a pang of grateful jealousy. He got together the things that Mrs. Kenton had pretended to want, and after glancing in at the different rooms, which seemed to be lying stealthily in wait for him, with their emptiness and silence, he went down-stairs with the bundle he had made, and turned into his library. He had some thought of looking at the collections for his history, but, after pulling open one of the drawers in which they were stored, he pushed it to again, and sank listlessly into his leather-covered swivel-chair, which stood in its place before the wide writing-table, and seemed to have had him in it before he sat down. The table was bare, except for the books and documents which he had sent home from time to time during the winter, and which Richard or his wife had neatly arranged there without breaking their wraps. He let fall his bundle at his feet, and sat staring at the ranks of books against the wall, mechanically relating them to the different epochs of the past in which he or his wife or his children had been interested in them, and aching with tender pain. He had always supposed himself a happy and strong and successful man, but what a dreary ruin his life had fallen into! Was it to be finally so helpless and powerless (for with all the defences about him that a man can have, he felt himself fatally vulnerable) that he had fought so many years? Why, at his age, should he be going into exile, away from everything that could make his days bright and sweet? Why could not he come back there, where he was now more solitary than he could be anywhere else on earth, and reanimate the dead body of his home with his old life? He knew why, in an immediate sort, but his quest was for the cause behind the cause. What had he done, or left undone? He had tried to be a just man, and fulfil all his duties both to his family and to his neighbors; he had wished to be kind, and not to harm any one; he reflected how, as he had grown older, the dread of doing any unkindness had grown upon him, and how he had tried not to be proud, but to walk meekly and humbly. Why should he be punished as he was, stricken in a place so sacred that the effort to defend himself had seemed a kind of sacrilege? He could not make it out, and he was not aware of the tears of self-pity that stole slowly down his face, though from time to time he wiped them away.

He heard steps in the hall without, advancing and pausing, which must be those of his son coming back for him, and with these advances and pauses giving him notice of his approach; but he did not move, and at first he did not look up when the steps arrived at the threshold of the room where he sat. When he lifted his eyes at last he saw Bittridge lounging in the doorway, with one shoulder supported against the door-jamb, his hands in his pockets and his hat pushed well back on his forehead. In an instant all Kenton's humility and soft repining were gone. "Well, what is it?" he called.

"Oh," said Bittridge, coming forward. He laughed and explained, "Didn't know if you recognized me."

"I recognized you," said Kenton, fiercely. "What is it you want?"

"Well, I happened to be passing, and I saw the door open, and I thought maybe Dick was here."

It was on Kenton's tongue to say that it was a good thing for him Dick was not there. But partly the sense that this would be unbecoming bluster, and partly the suffocating resentment of the fellow's impudence, limited his response to a formless gasp, and Bittridge went on: "But I'm glad to find you here, judge. I didn't know that you were in town. Family all well in New York?" He was not quelled by the silence of the judge on this point, but, as if he had not expected any definite reply to what might well pass for formal civility, he now looked aslant into his breast-pocket from which he drew a folded paper. "I just got hold of a document this morning that I think will interest you. I was bringing it round to Dick's wife for you." The intolerable familiarity of all this was fast working Kenton to a violent explosion, but he contained himself, and Bittridge stepped forward to lay the paper on the table before him. "It's the original roster of Company C, in your regiment, and -"

"Take it away!" shouted Kenton, "and take yourself away with it!" and he grasped the stick that shook in his hand.

A wicked light came into Bittridge's eye as he drawled, in lazy scorn, "Oh, I don't know." Then his truculence broke in a malicious amusement. "Why, judge, what's the matter?" He put on a face of mock gravity, and Kenton knew with helpless fury that he was enjoying his vantage. He could fall upon him and beat him with his stick, leaving the situation otherwise undefined, but a moment's reflection convinced Kenton that this would not do. It made him sick to think of striking the fellow, as if in that act he should be striking Ellen, too. It did not occur to him that he could be physically worsted, or that his vehement age would be no match for the other's vigorous youth. All he thought was that it would not avail, except to make known to every one what none but her dearest could now conjecture. Bittridge could then publicly say, and doubtless would say, that he had never made love to Ellen; that if there had been any love-making it was all on her side; and that he had only paid her the attentions which any young man might blamelessly pay a pretty girl. This would be true to the facts in the case, though it was true also that he had used every tacit art to make her believe him in love with her. But how could this truth be urged, and to whom? So far the affair had been quite in the hands of Ellen's family, and they had all acted for the best, up to the present time. They had given Bittridge no grievance in making him feel that he was unwelcome in their house, and they were quite within their rights in going away, and making it impossible for him to see her again anywhere in Tuskingum. As for his seeing her in New York, Ellen had but to say that she did not wish it, and that would end it. Now, however, by treating him rudely, Kenton was aware that he had bound himself to render Bittridge some account of his behavior throughout, if the fellow insisted upon it.

"I want nothing to do with you, sir," he said, less violently, but, as he felt, not more effectually. "You are in my house without my invitation, and against my wish!"

"I didn't expect to find you here. I came in because I saw the door open, and I thought I might see Dick or his wife and give them, this paper for you. But I'm glad I found you, and if you won't give me any reason for not wanting me here, I can give it myself, and I think I can make out a very good case for you." Kenton quivered in anticipation of some mention of Ellen, and Bittridge smiled as if he understood. But he went on to say: "I know that there were things happened after you first gave me the run of your house that might make you want to

William Dean Howells

put up the bars again - if they were true. But they were not true. And I can prove that by the best of all possible witnesses - by Uphill himself. He stands shoulder to shoulder with me, to make it hot for any one who couples his wife's name with mine."

"Humph!" Kenton could not help making this comment, and Bittridge, being what he was, could not help laughing.

"What's the use?" he asked, recovering himself. "I don't pretend that I did right, but you know there wasn't any harm in it. And if there had been I should have got the worst of it. Honestly, judge, I couldn't tell you how much I prized being admitted to your house on the terms I was. Don't you think I could appreciate the kindness you all showed me? Before you took me up, I was alone in Tuskingum, but you opened every door in the place for me. You made it home to me; and you won't believe it, of course, because you're prejudiced; but I felt like a son and brother to you all. I felt towards Mrs. Kenton just as I do towards my own mother. I lost the best friends I ever had when you turned against me. Don't you suppose I've seen the difference here in Tuskingum? Of course, the men pass the time of day with me when we meet, but they don't look me up, and there are more near-sighted girls in this town!" Kenton could not keep the remote dawn of a smile out of his eyes, and Bittridge caught the far-off gleam. "And everybody's been away the whole winter. Not a soul at home, anywhere, and I had to take my chance of surprising Mrs. Dick Kenton when I saw your door open here." He laughed forlornly, as the gleam faded out of Kenton's eye again. "And the worst of it is that my own mother isn't at home to me, figuratively speaking, when I go over to see her at Ballardsville. She got wind of my misfortune, somehow, and when I made a clean breast of it to her, she said she could never feel the same to me till I had made it all right with the Kentons. And when a man's own mother is down on him, judge!"

Bittridge left Kenton to imagine the desperate case, and in spite of his disbelief in the man and all he said, Kenton could not keep his hardness of heart towards him. "I don't know what you're after, young man," he began. "But if you expect me to receive you under my roof again -"

"Oh, I don't, judge, I don't!" Bittridge interposed. "All I want is to be able to tell my mother - I don't care for anybody else - that I saw you, and you allowed me to say that I was truly sorry for the pain - if it was pain; or annoyance, anyway - that I had caused you, and to go back to her with the hope of atoning for it sometime or somehow. That's all."

"Look here!" cried Renton. "What have you written to my daughter for?"

"Wasn't that natural? I prized her esteem more than I do yours even; but did I ask her anything more than I've asked you? I didn't expect her to answer me; all I wanted was to have her believe that I wasn't as black as I was painted - not inside, anyway. You know well enough - anybody knows - that I would rather have her think well of me than any one else in his world, except my mother. I haven't got the gift of showing out what's good in me, if there is any good, but I believe Miss Ellen would want to think well of me if I gave her a chance. If ever there was an angel on earth, she's one. I don't deny that I was hopeful of mercy from her, because she can't think evil, but I can lay my hand on my heart and say that I wasn't selfish in my hopes. It seemed to me that it was her due to understand that a man whom she had allowed to be her friend wasn't altogether unworthy. That's as near as I can come to putting into words the motive I had in writing to her. I can't even begin to put into words the feeling I have towards her. It's as if she was something sacred."

This was the feeling Renton himself had towards his daughter, and for the first time he found himself on common ground with the scapegrace who professed it, and whose light, mocking face so little enforced his profession. If Bittridge could have spoken in the dark, his words might have carried a conviction of his sincerity, but there, in plain day, confronting the father of Ellen, who had every wish to believe him true, the effect was different. Deep within his wish to think the man honest, Kenton recoiled from him. He vaguely perceived that it was because she could not think evil that this wretch had power upon her, and he was sensible, as he had not been before, that she had no safety from him except in absence. He did not know what to answer; he could not repel him in open terms, and still less could he meet him with any words that would allow him to resume his former relations with his family. He said, finally: "We will let matters stand. We are going to Europe in a week, and I shall not see you again. I will tell Mrs. Kenton what you say."

"Thank you, judge. And tell her that I appreciate your kindness more than I can say!" The judge rose from his chair and went towards the window, which he had thrown open. "Going to shut up? Let me help you with that window; it seems to stick. Everything fast up-stairs?"

"I - I think so," Kenton hesitated.

"I'll just run up and look," said Bittridge, and he took the stairs two at a time, before Kenton could protest, when they came out into the hall together. "It's all right," he reported on his quick return. "I'll just look round below here," and he explored the ground-floor rooms in turn. "No, you hadn't opened any other window," he said, glancing finally into the library. "Shall I leave this paper on your table?"

"Yes, leave it there," said Kenton, helplessly, and he let Bittridge close the front door after him, and lock it.

"I hope Miss Lottie is well," he suggested in handing the key to Kenton. "And Boyne" he added, with the cordiality of an old family friend. "I hope Boyne has got reconciled to New York a little. He was rather anxious about his pigeons when he left, I understand. But I guess Dick's man has looked after them. I'd have offered to take charge of the cocoons myself if I'd had a chance." He walked, gayly chatting, across the intervening lawn with Kenton to his son's door, where at sight of him bra. Richard Kenton evanesced into the interior so obviously that Bittridge could not offer to come in. "Well, I shall see you all when you come back in the fall, judge, and I hope you'll have a pleasant voyage and a good time in Europe."

"Thank you," said Kenton, briefly.

"Remember me to the ladies!" and Bittridge took off his hat with his left hand, while he offered the judge his right. "Well, good-bye!"

Kenton made what response he could, and escaped in-doors, where his daughter-in-law appeared from the obscurity into which she had retired from Bittridge. "Well, that follow does beat all! How, in the world did he find you, father?"

"He came into the house," said the judge, much abashed at his failure to deal adequately with Bittridge. He felt it the more in the presence of his son's wife. "I couldn't, seem to get rid of him in any way short of kicking him out."

"No, there's nothing equal to his impudence. I do believe he would have come in here, if he hadn't seen me first. Did you tell him when you were going back, father? Because he'd be at the train to see you off, just as sure!"

"No, I didn't tell him," said Kenton, feeling move shaken now from the interview with Bittridge than he had realized before. He was ashamed to let Mary know that he had listened to Bittridge's justification, which he now perceived was none, and he would have liked to pretend that he had not silently condoned his offences, but Mary did not drive him to these deceptions by any further allusions to Bittridge.

"Well, now, you must go into the sitting-room and lie down on the lounge; I promised Dick to make you. Or would you rather go up-stairs to your room?"

William Dean Howells

"I think I'll go to my room," said Kenton.

He was asleep there on the bed when Richard came home to dinner and looked softly in. He decided not to wake him, and Mary said the sleep would do him more good than the dinner. At table they talked him over, and she told her husband what she knew of the morning's adventure.

"That was pretty tough for father," said Richard. "I wouldn't go into the house with him, because I knew he wanted to have it to himself; and then to think of that dirty hound skulking in! Well, perhaps it's for the best. It will make it easier, for father to go and leave the place, and they've got to go. They've got to put the Atlantic Ocean between Ellen and that fellow."

"It does seem as if something might be done," his wife rebelled.

"They've done the best that could be done," said Richard. "And if that skunk hasn't got some sort of new hold upon father, I shall be satisfied. The worst of it is that it will be all over town in an hour that Bittridge has made up with us. I don't blame father; he couldn't help it; he never could be rude to anybody."

"I think I'll try if I can't be rude to Mr. Bittridge, if he ever undertakes to show in my pretence that he has made it up with us," said Mary.

Richard tenderly found out from his father's shamefaced reluctance, later, that no great mischief had been done. But no precaution on his part availed to keep Bittridge from demonstrating the good feeling between himself and the Kentons when the judge started for New York the next afternoon. He was there waiting to see him off, and he all but took the adieus out of Richard's hands. He got possession of the judge's valise, and pressed past the porter into the sleeping-car with it, and remained lounging on the arm of the judge's seat, making conversation with him and Richard till the train began to move. Then he ran outside, and waved his hand to the judge's window in farewell, before all that leisure of Tuskingum which haunted the arrival and departure of the trains.

Mary Kenton was furious when her husband came home and reported the fact to her.

"How in the world did he find out when father was going?"

"He must have come to all the through trains since he say him yesterday. But I think even you would have been suited, Mary, if you had seen his failure to walk off from the depot arm-in-arm with me:

"I wouldn't have been suited with anything short of your knocking, him down, Dick."

"Oh, that wouldn't have done," said Richard. After a while he added, patiently, "Ellen is making a good deal of trouble for us."

This was what Mary was thinking herself, and it was what she might have said, but since Dick had said it she was obliged to protest. "She isn't to blame for it."

"Oh, I know she isn't to blame."

V

The father of the unhappy girl was of the same mixed mind as he rode sleeplessly back to New York in his berth, and heard the noises of slumber all round him. From time to time he groaned softly, and turned from one cheek to the other. Every half-hour or so he let his window-curtain fly up, and lay watching the landscape fleeting past; and then he pulled the curtain down again and tried to sleep. After passing Albany he dozed, but at Poughkeepsie a zealous porter called him by mistake, and the rest of the way to New York he sat up in the smoking-room. It seemed a long while since he had drowsed; the thin nap had not rested him, and the old face that showed itself in the glass, with the frost of a two days' beard on it, was dry-eyed and limply squared by the fall of the muscles at the corners of the chin.

He wondered how he should justify to his wife the thing which he felt as accountable for having happened to him as if he could have prevented it. It would not have happened, of course, if he had not gone to Tuskingum, and she could say that to him; now it seemed to him that his going, which had been so imperative before he went, was altogether needless. Nothing but harm had come of it, and it had been a selfish indulgence of a culpable weakness.

It was a little better for Kenton when he found himself with his family, and they went down together to the breakfast which the mother had engaged the younger children to make as pleasant as they could for their father, and not worry him with talk about Tuskingum. They had, in fact, got over their first season of homesickness, and were postponing their longing for Tuskingum till their return from Europe, when they would all go straight out there. Kenton ran the gauntlet of welcome from the black elevator-boys and bell-boys and the head-waiter, who went before him to pull out the judge's chair, with commanding frowns to his underlings to do the like for the rest of the family; and as his own clumsy Irish waiter stood behind his chair, breathing heavily upon the judge's head, he gave his order for breakfast, with a curious sense of having got home again from some strange place. He satisfied Boyne that his pigeons and poultry had been well cared for through the winter, and he told Lottie that he had not met much of anybody except Dick's family, before he recollected seeing half a dozen of her young men at differed times. She was not very exacting about them and her mind seemed set upon Europe, or at least she talked of nothing else. Ellen was quiet as she always was, but she smiled gently on her father, and Mrs. Kenton told him of the girl's preparations for going, and congratulated herself on their wisdom in having postponed their sailing, in view of all they had to do; and she made Kenton feel that everything was in the best possible shape. As soon as she got him alone in their own room, she said, "Well, what is it, poppa?"

Then he had to tell her, and she listened with ominous gravity. She did not say that now he could see how much better it would have been if he had not gone, but she made him say it for her; and she would not let him take comfort in the notion of keeping the fact of his interview with Bittridge from Ellen. "It would be worse than useless. He will write to her about it, and then she will know that we have been, concealing it."

Kenton was astonished at himself for not having thought of that. "And what are you going to do, Sarah?"

"I am going to tell her," said Mrs. Kenton.

"Why didn't poppa tell me before?" the girl perversely

demanded, as soon as her another had done so.

"Ellen, you are a naughty child! I have a great mind not to have a word more to say to you. Your father hasn't been in the house an hour. Did you want him to speak before Lottie and Boyne!"

"I don't see why he didn't tell me himself. I know there is something you are keeping back. I know there is some word -"

"Oh, you poor girl!" said her mother, melting into pity against all sense of duty. "Have we ever tried to deceive you?"

"No," Ellen sobbed, with her face in her hands. "Now I will tell you every word that passed," said Mrs. Kenton, and she told, as well as she could remember, all that the judge had repeated from Bittridge. "I don't say he isn't ashamed of himself," she commented at the end. "He ought to be, and, of course, he would be glad to be in with us again when we go back; but that doesn't alter his character, Ellen. Still, if you can't see that yourself, I don't want to make you, and if you would rather go home to Tuskingum, we will give up the trip to Europe."

"It's too late to do that now," said the girl, in cruel reproach.

Her mother closed her lips resolutely till she could say, "Or you can write to him if you want to."

"I don't want to," said Ellen, and she dragged herself up out of her chair, and trailed slowly out of the room without looking at her mother.

"Well?" the judge asked, impatiently, when he came in as soon after this as he decently could. They observed forms with regard to talking about Ellen which, after all, were rather for themselves than for her; Mrs. Kenton, at least, knew that the girl knew when they were talking about her.

"She took it as well as I expected."

"What is she going to do?"

"She didn't say. But I don't believe she will do anything."

"I wish I had taken our tickets for next Saturday," said Kenton.

"Well, we must wait now," said his wife. "If he doesn't write to her, she won't write to him."

"Has she ever answered that letter of his?"

"No, and I don't believe she will now."

That night Ellen came to her mother and said she need not be afraid of her writing to Bittridge. "He hasn't changed, if he was wrong, by coming and saying those things to poppa, and nothing has changed."

"That is the way I hoped you would see it; Ellen." Her mother looked wistfully at her, but the girl left her without letting her satisfy the longing in the mother's heart to put her arms round her child, and pull her head down upon her breast for a cry.

Kenton slept better that night than his wife, who was kept awake by a formless foreboding. For the week that followed she had the sense of literally pushing the hours away, so that at times she found herself breathless, as if from some heavy physical exertion. At such times she was frantic with the wish to have the days gone, and the day of their sailing come, but she kept her impatience from her husband and children, and especially from Ellen. The girl was passive enough; she was almost willing, and in the preparation for their voyage she did her share of the shopping, and discussed the difficult points of this business with her mother and sister as if she had really been thinking about it all. But her mother doubted if she had, and made more of Ellen's sunken eyes and thin face than of her intelligent and attentive words. It was these that she reported to her husband, whom she kept from talking with Ellen, and otherwise quelled.

"Let her alone," she insisted, one morning of the last week. "What can you do by speaking to her about it? Don't you see that she is making the best fight she can? You will weaken her if you interfere. It's less than a week now, and if you can only hold out, I know she can."

Kenton groaned. "Well, I suppose you're right, Sarah. But I don't like the idea of forcing her to go, unless -"

"Then you had better write to that fellow, and ask him to come and get her."

This shut Kenton's mouth, and he kept on with his shaving. When he had finished he felt fresher, if not stronger, and he went down to breakfast, which he had alone, not only with reference to his own family, but all the other guests of the hotel. He was always so early that sometimes the dining-room was not open; when this happened, he used to go and buy a newspaper at the clerk's desk, for it was too early then for the news-stand to be open. It happened so that morning, and he got his paper without noticing the young man who was writing his name in the hotel register, but who looked briskly up when the clerk bade Kenton good-morning by name.

"Why, judge!" he said, and he put out a hand which Kenton took with trembling reluctance and a dazed stare. "I thought you sailed last Saturday!"

"We sail next Saturday," said Kenton.

"Well, well! Then I misunderstood," said Bittridge, and he added: "Why, this is money found in the road! How are all the family? I've got my mother here with me; brought her on for a kind of a little outing. She'll be the most surprised woman in New York when I tell her you're here yet. We came to this hotel because we knew you had been here, but we didn't suppose you were here! Well! This is too good! I saw Dick, Friday, but he didn't say anything about your sailing; I suppose he thought I knew. Didn't you tell me you were going in a week, that day in your house?"

"Perhaps I did," Kenton faltered out, his eyes fixed on Bittridge's with a helpless fascination.

"Well, it don't matter so long as you're here. Mother's in the parlor waiting for me; I won't risk taking you to her now, judge - right off the train, you know. But I want to bring her to call on Mrs. Kenton as soon after breakfast as you'll let me. She just idolizes Mrs. Kenton, from what I've told her about her. Our rooms ready?" He turned to the clerk, and the clerk called "Front!" to a bellboy, who ran up and took Bittridge's hand-baggage, and stood waiting to follow him into the parlor. "Well, you must excuse me now, judge. So long!" he said, gayly, and Kenton crept feebly away to the dining-room.

He must have eaten breakfast, but he was not aware of doing so; and the events of his leaving the table and going up in the elevator and finding himself in his wife's presence did not present themselves consecutively, though they must all have successively occurred. It did not seem to him that he could tell what he knew, but he found himself doing it, and her hearing it with strange quiet.

"Very well," she said. "I must tell Ellen, and, if she wishes, we must stay in and wait for their call."

"Yes," the judge mechanically consented.

It was painful for Mrs. Kenton to see how the girl flushed when she announced the fact of Bittridge's presence, for she knew what a strife of hope and shame and pride there was in Ellen's heart. At first she said that she did not wish to see him, and then when Mrs. Kenton would not say whether she had better see him or not, she added, vaguely, "If he has brought his mother -"

"I think we must see them, Ellen. You wouldn't wish to think you had been unkind; and he might be hurt on his mother's account. He seems really fond of her, and perhaps -"

"No, there isn't any perhaps, momma," said the girl, gratefully. "But I think we had better see them, too. I think we had better ALL see them."

"Just as you please, Ellen. If you prefer to meet them alone -"

"I don't prefer that. I want poppa to be there, and Lottie and Boyne even."

Boyne objected when he was told that his presence was requested at this family rite, and he would have excused himself if the invitation had been of the form that one might decline. "What do I want to see him for?" he puffed. "He never cared anything about me in Tuskingum. What's he want here, anyway?"

"I wish you to come in, my son," said his mother, and that ended it.

Lottie was not so tractable. "Very well, momma," she said. "But don't expect me to speak to him. I have some little self-respect, if the rest of you haven't. Am I going to shake hands with him! I never took the least notice of him at home, and I'm not going to here."

Bittridge decided the question of hand-shaking for her when they met. He greeted her glooming brother with a jolly "Hello, Boyne!" and without waiting for the boy's tardy response he said "Hello, Lottie!" to the girl, and took her hand and kept it in his while he made an elaborate compliment to her good looks and her gain in weight. She had come tardily as a proof that she would not have come in at all if she had not chosen to do so, and Mrs. Bittridge was already seated beside Ellen on the sofa, holding her hand, and trying to keep her mobile, inattentive eyes upon Ellen's face. She was a little woman, youthfully dressed, but not dressed youthfully enough for the dry, yellow hair which curled tightly in small rings on her skull, like the wig of a rag-doll. Her restless eyes were round and deep-set, with the lids flung up out of sight; she had a lax, formless mouth, and an anxious smile, with which she constantly watched her son for his initiative, while she recollected herself from time to time, long enough to smooth Ellen's hand between her own, and say, "Oh, I just think the world of Clarence; and I guess he thinks his mother is about right, too," and then did not heed what Ellen answered.

The girl said very little, and it was Bittridge who talked for all, dominating the room with a large, satisfied presence, in which the judge sat withdrawn, his forehead supported on his hand, and his elbow on the table. Mrs. Kenton held herself upright, with her hands crossed before her, stealing a look now and then at her daughter's averted face, but keeping her eyes from Mrs. Bittridge, who, whenever she caught Mrs. Kenton's glance, said something to her about her Clarence, and how he used to write home to her at Ballardsville about the Kentons, so that she felt acquainted with all of them. Her reminiscences were perfunctory; Mrs. Bittridge had voluntarily but one topic, and that was herself, either as she was included in the interest her son must inspire, or as she included him in the interest she must inspire. She said that, now they had met at last, she was not going to rest till the Kentons had been over to Ballardsville, and made her a good, long visit; her son had some difficulty in making her realize that the Kentons were going to Europe. Then she laughed, and said she kept forgetting; and she did wish they were all coming back to Tuskingum.

If it is a merit to treat a fatuous mother with deference, Bittridge had that merit. His deference was of the caressing and laughing sort, which took the spectator into the joke of her peculiarities as something they would appreciate and enjoy with him. She had been a kittenish and petted person in her youth, perhaps, and now she petted herself, after she had long ceased to be a kitten. What was respectable and what was

William Dean Howells

pathetic in her was her wish to promote her son's fortunes with the Kentons, but she tried to do this from not a very clear understanding of her part, apparently, and little sense of the means. For Ellen's sake, rather than hers, the father and mother received her overtures to their liking kindly; they answered her patiently, and Mrs. Kenton even tried to lead the way for her to show herself at her best, by talking of her journey on to New York, and of the city, and what she would see there to interest her. Lottie and Boyne, sternly aloof together in one of their momentary alliances, listened to her replies with a silent contempt that almost included their mother; Kenton bore with the woman humbly and sadly.

He was, in fact, rather bewildered with the situation, for which he felt himself remotely if not immediately responsible. Bittridge was there among them not only on good terms, but apparently in the character of a more than tolerated pretendant to Ellen's favor. There were passages of time is which the father was not sure that the fellow was not engaged to his daughter, though when these instants were gone he was aware that there had been no overt love-making between them and Bittridge had never offered himself. What was he doing there, then? The judge asked himself that, without being able to answer himself. So far as he could make out, his wife and he were letting him see Ellen, and show her off to his mother, mainly to disgust her with them both, and because they were afraid that if they denied her to him, it would be the worse for them through her suffering. The judge was not accustomed to apply the tests by which people are found vulgar or not; these were not of his simple world; all that he felt about Mrs. Bittridge was that she was a very foolish, false person, who was true in nothing but her admiration of her rascal of a son; he did not think of Bittridge as a rascal violently, but helplessly, and with a heart that melted in pity for Ellen.

He longed to have these people gone, not so much because he was so unhappy in their presence as because he wished to learn Ellen's feeling about them from his wife. She would know, whether Allen said anything to her or not. But perhaps if Mrs.

Kenton had been asked to deliver her mind on this point at once she would have been a little puled. All that she could see, and she saw it with a sinking of the heart, was that Ellen looked more at peace than she had been since Bittridge was last in their house at Tuskingum. Her eyes covertly followed him as he sat talking, or went about the room, making himself at home among them, as if he were welcome with every one. He joked her more than the rest, and accused her of having become a regular New-Yorker; he said he supposed that when she came back from Europe she would not know anybody in Tuskingum; and his mother, playing with Ellen's fingers, as if they had been the fringe of a tassel, declared that she must not mind him, for he carried on just so with everybody; at the same time she ordered him to stop, or she would go right out of the room.

She gave no other sign of going, and it was her son who had to make the movement for her at last; she apparently did not know that it was her part to make it. She said that now the Kentons must come and return her call, and be real neighborly, just the same as if they were all at home together. When her son shook hands with every one she did so too, and she said to each, "Well, I wish you good-morning," and let him push her before him, in high delight with the joke, out of the room.

When they were gone the Kentons sat silent, Ellen with a rapt smile on her thin, flushed face, till Lottie said, "You forgot to ask him if we might BREATHE, poppa," and paced out of the room in stately scorn, followed by Boyne, who had apparently no words at the command of his dumb rage. Kenton wished to remain, and he looked at his wife for instruction. She frowned, and he took this for a sign that he had better go, and he went with a light sigh.

He did not know what else to do with himself, and he went down to the reading-room. He found Bittridge there, smoking a cigar, and the young man companionably offered to bestow one upon him; but the judge stiffly refused, saying he did not

William Dean Howells

wish to smoke just then. He noted that Bittridge was still in his character of family favorite, and his hand trembled as he passed it over the smooth knob of his stick, while he sat waiting for the fellow to take himself away. But Bittridge had apparently no thought of going. He was looking at the amusements for the evening in a paper he had bought, and he wished to consult the judge as to which was the best theatre to go to that night; he said he wanted to take his mother. Kenton professed not to know much about the New York theatres, and then Bittridge guessed he must get the clerk to tell him. But still he did not part with the judge. He sat down beside him, and told him how glad he was to see his family looking so well, especially Miss Ellen; he could not remember ever seeing her so strong-looking. He said that girl had captured his mother, who was in love with pretty much the whole Kenton family, though.

"And by-the-way," he added, "I want to thank you and Mrs. Kenton, judge, for the way you received my mother. You made her feel that she was among friends. She can't talk about anything else, and I guess I sha'n't have much trouble in making her stay in New York as long as you're here. She was inclined to be homesick. The fact is, though I don't care to have it talked about yet, and I wish you wouldn't say anything to Dick about it when you write home, I think of settling in New York. I've been offered a show in the advertising department of one of the big dailies - I'm not at liberty to say which - and it's a toss-up whether I stay here or go to Washington; I've got a chance there, too, but it's on the staff of a new enterprise, and I'm not sure about it. I've brought my mother along to let her have a look at both places, though she doesn't know it, and I'd rather you wouldn't speak of it before her; I'm going to take her on to Washington before we go back. I want to have my mother with me, judge. It's better for a fellow to have that home-feeling in a large place from the start; it keeps him out of a lot of things, and I don't pretend to be better than other people, or not more superhuman. If I've been able to keep out of scrapes, it's more because I've had my mother near me, and I don't intend ever to be separated from her, after this, till I have a home of my own. She's been the guiding-star of my life."

Kenton was unable to make any formal response, and, in fact, he was so preoccupied with the question whether the fellow was more a fool or a fraud that he made no answer at all, beyond a few inarticulate grumblings of assent. These sufficed for Bittridge, apparently, for he went on contentedly: "Whenever I've been tempted to go a little wild, the thought of how mother would feel has kept me on the track like nothing else would. No, judge, there isn't anything in this world like a good mother, except the right kind of a wife."

Kenton rose, and said he believed he must go upstairs. Bittridge said, "All right; I'll see you later, judge," and swung easily off to advise with the clerk as to the best theatre.

VI

Kenton was so unhappy that he could not wait for his wife to come to him in their own room; he broke in upon her and Ellen in the parlor, and at his coming the girl flitted out, in the noiseless fashion which of late had made her father feel something ghostlike in her. He was afraid she was growing to dislike him, and trying to avoid him, and now he presented himself quite humbly before his wife, as if he had done wrong in coming. He began with a sort of apology for interrupting, but his wife said it was all right, and she added, "We were not talking about anything in particular." She was silent, and then she added again: "Sometimes I think Ellen hasn't very fine perceptions, after all. She doesn't seem to feel about people as I supposed she would."

"You mean that she doesn't feel as you would suppose about those people?"

Mrs. Kenton answered, obliquely. "She thinks it's a beautiful thing in him to be so devoted to his mother."

"Humph! And what does she think of his mother?"

"She thinks she has very pretty hair."

Mrs. Kenton looked gravely down at the work she had in her hands, and Kenton did not know what to make of it all. He decided that his wife must feel, as he did, a doubt of the child's sincerity, with sense of her evasiveness more tolerant than his own. Yet he knew that if it came to a question of forcing Ellen to do what was best for her, or forbidding her to do what was worst, his wife would have all the strength for the work, and he none. He asked her, hopelessly enough, "Do you think she still cares for him?"

"I think she wishes to give him another trial; I hope she will." Kenton was daunted, and he showed it. "She has got to convince herself, and we have got to let her. She believes, of course, that he's here on her account, and that flatters her. Why should she be so different from other girls?" Mrs. Kenton demanded of the angry protest in her husband's eye.

His spirit fell, and he said, "I only wish she were more like them."

"Well, then, she is just as headstrong and as silly, when it comes to a thing like this. Our only hope is to let her have her own way."

"Do you suppose he cares for her, after all?"

Mrs. Kenton was silent, as if in exhaustive self-question. Then she answered: "No, I don't in that way. But he believes he can get her."

"Then, Sarah, I think we have a duty to the poor child. You must tell her what you have told me."

Mrs. Kenton smiled rather bitterly, in recognition of the fact that the performance of their common duty must fall wholly to her. But she merely said: "There is no need of my telling her. She knows it already."

"And she would take him in spite of knowing that he didn't really care for her?"

"I don't say that. She wouldn't own it to herself."

"And what are you going to do?"

"Nothing. We must let things take their course."

They had a great deal more talk that came to the same end. They played their sad comedy, he in the part of a father determined to save his child from herself, and she in hers of resisting and withholding him. It ended as it had so often ended before - he yielded, with more faith in her wisdom than she had herself.

At luncheon the Bittridges could not join the Kentons, or be asked to do so, because the table held only four, but they stopped on their way to their own table, the mother to bridle and toss in affected reluctance, while the son bragged how he had got the last two tickets to be had that night for the theatre where he was going to take his mother. He seemed to think that the fact had a special claim on the judge's interest, and she to wish to find out whether Mrs. Kenton approved of theatre-going. She said she would not think of going in Ballardsville, but she supposed it was more rulable in New York.

During the afternoon she called at the Kenton apartment to consult the ladies about what she ought to wear. She said she had nothing but a black 'barege' along, and would that do with the hat she had on? She had worn it to let them see, and now she turned her face from aide to side to give them the effect of the plumes, that fell like a dishevelled feather-duster round and over the crown. Mrs. Kenton could only say that it would do, but she believed that it was the custom now for ladies to take their hats off in the theatre.

Mrs. Bittridge gave a hoarse laugh. "Oh, dear! Then I'll have to fix my hair two ways? I don't know what Clarence WILL say."

The mention of her son's name opened the way for her to talk of him in relation to herself, and the rest of her stay passed in the celebration of his filial virtues, which had been manifest from the earliest period. She could not remember that she ever had to hit the child a lick, she said, or that he had ever made her shed a tear.

When she went, Boyne gloomily inquired, "What makes her hair so much darker at the roots than it is at the points?" and his mother snubbed him promptly.

"You had no business to be here, Boyne. I don't like boys hanging about where ladies are talking together, and listening."

This did not prevent Lottie from answering, directly for Boyne, and indirectly for Ellen, "It's because it's begun to grow since the last bleach."

It was easier to grapple with Boyne than with Lottie, and Mrs. Kenton was willing to allow her to leave the room with her brother unrebuked. She was even willing to have had the veil lifted from Mrs. Bittridge's hair with a rude hand, if it world help Ellen.

"I don't want you to think, momma," said the girl, "that I didn't know about her hair, or that I don't see how silly she is. But it's all the more to his credit if he can be so good to her, and admire her. Would you like him better if he despised her?"

Mrs. Kenton felt both the defiance and the secret shame from which it sprang in her daughter's words; and she waited for a moment before she answered, "I would like to be sure he didn't!"

"If he does, and if he hides it from her, it's the same as if he didn't; it's better. But you all wish to dislike him."

"We don't wish to dislike him, Ellen, goodness knows. But I don't think he would care much whether we disliked him or not. I am sure your poor father and I would be only too glad to like him."

"Lottie wouldn't," said Ellen, with a resentment her mother found pathetic, it was so feeble and aimless.

"Lottie doesn't matter," she said. She could not make out how nearly Ellen was to sharing the common dislike, or how far she would go in fortifying herself against it. She kept with difficulty to her negative frankness, and she let the girl leave the room with a fretful sigh, as if provoked that her mother would not provoke her further. There were moments when Mrs. Kenton believed that Ellen was sick of her love, and that she would pluck it out of her heart herself if she were left alone. She was then glad Bittridge had come, so that Ellen might compare with the reality the counterfeit presentment she had kept in her fancy; and she believed that if she could but leave him to do his worst, it would be the best for Ellen.

In the evening, directly after dinner, Bittridge sent up his name for Mrs. Kenton. The judge had remained to read his paper below, and Lottie and Boyne had gone to some friends in another apartment. It seemed to Mrs. Kenton a piece of luck that she should be able to see him alone, and she could not have said that she was unprepared for him to come in, holding his theatre-tickets explanatorily in his hand, or surprised when he began:

"Mrs. Kenton, my mother's got a bad headache, and I've come to ask a favor of you. She can't use her ticket for to-night, and I want you to let Miss Ellen come with me. Will you?"

Bittridge had constituted himself an old friend of the whole family from the renewal of their acquaintance, and Mrs. Kenton was now made aware of his being her peculiar favorite, in spite of the instant repulsion she felt, she was not averse to what he proposed. Her fear was that Ellen would be so, or that she could keep from influencing her to this test of her real feeling for Bittridge. "I will ask her, Mr. Bittridge," she said, with a severity which was a preliminary of the impartiality she meant to use with Ellen.

"Well, that's right," he answered, and while she went to the girl's room he remained examining the details of the drawing-room decorations in easy security, which Mrs. Kenton justified on her return.

"Ellen will be ready to go with you, Mr. Bittridge."

"Well, that's good," said the young man, and while he talked on she sat wondering at a nature which all modesty and deference seemed left out of, though he had sometimes given evidence of his intellectual appreciation of these things. He talked to Mrs. Kenton not only as if they were in every-wise equal, but as if they were of the same age, almost of the same sex.

Ellen came in, cloaked and hatted, with her delicate face excited in prospect of the adventure; and her mother saw Bittridge look at her with more tenderness than she had ever seen in him before. "I'll take good care of her, Mrs. Kenton," he said, and for the first time she felt herself relent a little towards him.

A minute after they were gone Lottie bounced into the room, followed by Boyne.

"Momma!" she shouted, "Ellen isn't going to the theatre with that fellow?"

"Yes, she is."

"And you let her, momma! Without a chaperon?"

Boyne's face had mirrored the indignation in his sister's, but at this unprecedented burst of conventionality he forgot their momentary alliance. "Well, you're a pretty one to talk about chaperons! Walking all over Tuskingum with fellows at night, and going buggy-riding with everybody, and out rowing, and here fairly begging Jim Plumpton to come down to the steamer and see you off again!"

"Shut up!" Lottie violently returned, "or I'll tell momma how you've been behaving with Rita Plumpton yourself."

"Well, tell!" Boyne defied her.

"Oh, it don't matter what a brat of a boy says or does, anyway," said Lottie. "But I think Ellen is disgracing the family. Everybody in the hotel is laughing at that wiggy old Mrs. Bittridge, with her wobbly eyes, and they can see that he's just as green! The Plumptons have been laughing so about them, and I told them that we had nothing to do with them at home, and had fairly turned Bittridge out of the house, but he had impudence enough for anything; and now to find Ellen going off to the theatre with him alone!"

Lottie began to cry with vexation as she whipped out of the room, and Boyne, who felt himself drawn to her side again, said, very seriously: "Well, it ain't the thing in New York, you know, momma; and anybody can see what a jay Bittridge is. I think it's too bad to let her."

"It isn't for you to criticise your mother, Boyne," said Mrs. Kenton, but she was more shaken than she would allow. Her own traditions were so simple that the point of etiquette which her children had urged had not occurred to her. The question whether Ellen should go with Bittridge at all being decided, she would, of course, go in New York as she would go in Tuskingum. Now Mrs. Kenton perceived that she must not, and she had her share of humiliation in the impression which his mother, as her friend, apparently, was making with her children's acquaintances in the hotel. If they would think everybody in Tuskingum was like her, it would certainly be very unpleasant, but she would not quite own this to herself, still less to a fourteen-year-old boy. "I think what your father and I decide to be right will be sufficient excuse for you with your friends."

"Does father know it?" Boyne asked, most unexpectedly.

Having no other answer ready, Mrs. Kenton said, "You had better go to bed, my son."

"Well," he grumbled, as he left the room, "I don't know where all the pride of the Kentons is gone to."

In his sense of fallen greatness he attempted to join Lottie in her room, but she said, "Go away, nasty thing!" and Boyne was obliged to seek his own room, where he occupied himself with a contrivance he was inventing to enable you to close your door and turn off your gas by a system of pulleys without leaving your bed, when you were tired of reading.

Mrs. Kenton waited for her husband in much less comfort, and when he came, and asked, restlessly, "Where are the children?" she first told him that Lottie and Boyne were in their rooms before she could bring herself to say that Ellen had gone to the theatre with Bittridge.

It was some relief to have him take it in the dull way he did, and to say nothing worse than, "Did you think it was well to have her!"

"You may be sure I didn't want her to. But what would she have said if I had refused to let her go? I can tell you it isn't an easy matter to manage her in this business, and it's very easy for you to criticise, without taking the responsibility."

"I'm not criticising," said Kenton. "I know you have acted for the best."

"The children," said Mrs. Kenton, wishing to be justified further, "think she ought to have had a chaperon. I didn't think of that; it isn't the custom at home; but Lottie was very saucy about it, and I had to send Boyne to bed. I don't think our children are very much comfort to us."

"They are good children," Kenton said, said - provisionally.

"Yes, that is the worst of it. If they were bad, we wouldn't expect any comfort from them. Ellen is about perfect. She's as near an angel as a child can be, but she could hardly have given us more anxiety if she had been the worst girl in the world."

"That's true," the father sadly assented.

"She didn't really want to go with him to-night, I'll say that for her, and if I had said a single word against it she wouldn't have gone. But all at once, while she sat there trying to think how I could excuse her, she began asking me what she should wear. There's something strange about it, Rufus. If I believed in hypnotism, I should say she had gone because he willed her to go."

"I guess she went because she wanted to go because she's in love with him," said Kenton, hopelessly.

"Yes," Mrs. Kenton agreed. "I don't see how she can endure the sight of him. He's handsome enough," she added, with a woman's subjective logic. "And there's something fascinating about him. He's very graceful, and he's got a good figure."

"He's a hound!" said Kenton, exhaustively.

"Oh yes, he's a hound," she sighed, as if there could be no doubt on that point. "It don't seem right for him to be in the same room with Ellen. But it's for her to say. I feel more and more that we can't interfere without doing harm. I suppose that if she were not so innocent herself she would realize what he was better. But I do think he appreciates her innocence. He shows more reverence for her than for any one else."

"How was it his mother didn't go?" asked Kenton.

"She had a headache, he said. But I don't believe that. He always intended to get Ellen to go. And that's another thing Lottie was vexed about; she says everybody is laughing at Mrs. Bittridge, and it's mortifying to have people take her for a friend of ours."

"If there were nothing worse than that," said Kenton, "I guess we could live through it. Well, I don't know how it's going to all end."

They sat talking sadly, but finding a certain comfort in their mutual discouragement, and in their knowledge that they were doing the best they could for their child, whose freedom they must not infringe so far as to do what was absolutely best; and the time passed not so heavily till her return. This was announced by the mounting of the elevator to their landing, and then by low, rapid pleading in a man's voice outside. Kenton was about to open the door, when there came the formless noise of what seemed a struggle, and Ellen's voice rose in a muffed cry: "Oh! Oh! Let me be! Go away! I hate you!" Kenton the door open, and Ellen burst in, running to hide her face in her mother's breast, where she sobbed out, "He - he kissed me!" like a terrified child more than an insulted woman. Through the open door came the clatter of Bittridge's feet as he ran down-stairs.

VII

When Mrs. Kenton came from quieting the hysterical girl in her room she had the task, almost as delicate and difficult, of quieting her husband. She had kept him, by the most solemn and exhaustive entreaty, from following Bittridge downstairs and beating him with his stick, and now she was answerable to him for his forbearance. "If you don't behave yourself, Rufus," she had to say, "you will have some sort of stroke. After all, there's no harm done."

"No harm! Do you call it no harm for that hound to kiss Ellen?"

"He wouldn't have attempted it unless something had led up to it, I suppose."

"Sarah! How can you speak so of that angel?"

"Oh, that angel is a girl like the rest. You kissed me before we were engaged."

"That was very different."

"I don't see how. If your daughter is so sacred, why wasn't her mother? You men don't think your wives are sacred. That's it!"

"No, no, Sarah! It's because I don't think of you as apart from myself, that I can't think of you as I do of Ellen. I beg your pardon if I seemed to set her above you. But when I kissed you we were very young, and we lived in a simple day, when such things meant no harm; and I was very fond of you, and you were the holiest thing in the world to me. Is Ellen holy to that fellow?"

"I know," Mrs. Kenton relented. "I'm not comparing him to you. And there is a difference with Ellen. She isn't like other girls. If it had been Lottie -"

"I shouldn't have liked it with Lottie, either," said the major, stiffly. "But if it had been Lottie she would have boxed his ears for him, instead of running to you. Lottie can take care of herself. And I will take care of Ellen. When I see that scoundrel in the morning -"

"What will you do, an old man like you! I can tell you, it's something you've just got to bear it if you don't want the scandal to fill the whole hotel. It's a very fortunate thing, after all. It'll put an end to the whole affair."

"Do you think so, Sarah? If I believed that. What does Ellen say?"

"Nothing; she won't say anything - just cries and hides her face. I believe she is ashamed of having made a scene before us. But I know that she's so disgusted with him that she will never look at him again, and if it's brought her to that I should think his kissing her the greatest blessing in the world to us all. Yes, Ellen!"

Mrs. Kenton hurried off at a faint call from the girl's room, and when she came again she sat down to a long discussion of the situation with her husband, while she slowly took down her hair and prepared it for the night. Her conclusion, which she made her husband's, was that it was most fortunate they should be sailing so soon, and that it was the greatest pity they were not sailing in the morning. She wished him to sleep, whether she slept herself or not, and she put the most hopeful face possible upon the matter. "One thing you can rest assured of, Rufus, and that is that it's all over with Ellen. She may never speak to you about him, and you mustn't ever mention him, but she feels just as you could wish. Does that satisfy you? Some time I will tell you all she says."

"I don't care to hear," said Kenton. "All I want is for him to keep away from me. I think if he spoke to me I should kill him."

"Rufus!"

"I can't help it, Sarah. I feel outraged to the bottom of my soul. I could kill him."

Mrs. Kenton turned her head and looked steadfastly at him over her shoulder. "If you strike him, if you touch him, Mr. Kenton, you will undo everything that the abominable wretch has done for Ellen, and you will close my mouth and tie my hands. Will you promise that under no provocation whatever will you do him the least harm? I know Ellen better than you do, and I know that you will make her hate you unless -"

"Oh, I will promise. You needn't be afraid. Lord help me!" Kenton groaned. "I won't touch him. But don't expect me to speak to him."

"No, I don't expect that. He won't offer to speak to you."

They slept, and in the morning she stayed to breakfast with Ellen in their apartment, and let her husband go down with their younger children. She could trust him now, whatever form his further trial should take, and he felt that he was pledging himself to her anew, when Bittridge came hilariously to meet him in the reading-room, where he went for a paper after breakfast.

"Ah, judge!" said the young man, gayly. "Hello, Boyne!" he added to the boy, who had come with his father; Lottie had gone directly up-stairs from the breakfast-room. "I hope you're all well this morning? Play not too much for Miss Ellen?"

Kenton looked him in the face without answering, and then tried to get away from him, but Bittridge followed him up, talking, and ignoring his silence.

"It was a splendid piece, judge. You must take Mrs. Kenton. I know you'll both like it. I haven't ever seen Miss Ellen so interested. I hope the walk home didn't fatigue her. I wanted to get a cab, but she would walk." The judge kept moving on, with his head down. He did not speak, and Bittridge was forced to notice his silence. "Nothing the matter, I hope, with Miss Ellen, judge?"

"Go away," said the judge, in a low voice, fumbling the head of his stick.

"Why, what's up?" asked Bittridge, and he managed to get in front of Kenton and stay him at a point where Kenton could not escape. It was a corner of the room to which the old man had aimlessly tended, with no purpose but to avoid him:

"I wish you to let me alone, sir," said Kenton at last. "I can't speak to you."

"I understand what you mean, judge," said Bittridge, with a grin, all the more maddening because it seemed involuntary. "But I can explain everything. I just want a few words with you. It's very important; it's life or death with me, sir," he said, trying to look grave. "Will you let me go to your rooms with you?"

Kenton made no reply.

Bittridge began to laugh. "Then let's sit down here, or in the ladies' parlor. It won't take me two minutes to make everything right. If you don't believe I'm in earnest I know you don't think I am, but I can assure you - Will you let me speak with you about Miss Ellen?"

William Dean Howells

Still Kenton did not answer, shutting his lips tight, and remembering his promise to his wife.

Bittridge laughed, as if in amusement at what he had done. "Judge, let me say two words to you in private! If you can't now, tell me when you can. We're going back this evening, mother and I are; she isn't well, and I'm not going to take her to Washington. I don't want to go leaving you with the idea that I wanted to insult Miss Ellen. I care too much for her. I want to see you and Mrs. Kenton about it. I do, indeed. And won't you let me see you, somewhere?"

Kenton looked away, first to one side and then to another, and seemed stifling.

"Won't you speak to me! Won't you answer me? See here! I'd get down on my knees to you if it would do you any good. Where will you talk with me?"

"Nowhere!" shouted Kenton. "Will you go away, or shall I strike you with my stick?"

"Oh, I don't think," said Bittridge, and suddenly, in the wantonness of his baffled effrontery, he raised his hand and rubbed the back of it in the old man's face.

Boyne Kenton struck wildly at him, and Bittridge caught the boy by the arm and flung him to his knees on the marble floor. The men reading in the arm-chairs about started to their feet; a porter came running, and took hold of Bittridge. "Do you want an officer, Judge Kenton?" he panted.

"No, no!" Kenton answered, choking and trembling. "Don't arrest him. I wish to go to my rooms, that's all. Let him go. Don't do anything about it."

"I'll help you, judge," said the porter. "Take hold of this fellow," he said to two other porters who came up. "Take him to the desk, and tell the clerk he struck Judge Kenton, but the judge don't want him arrested."

Before Kenton reached the elevator with Boyne, who was rubbing his knees and fighting back the tears, he heard the clerk's voice saying, formally, to the porters, "Baggage out of 35 and 37" and adding, as mechanically, to Bittridge: "Your rooms are wanted. Get out of them at once!"

It seemed the gathering of neighborhood about Kenton, where he had felt himself so unfriended, against the outrage done him, and he felt the sweetness of being personally championed in a place where he had thought himself valued merely for the profit that was in him; his eyes filled, and his voice failed him in thanking the elevator-boy for running before him to ring the bell of his apartment.

VIII

The next day, in Tuskingum, Richard, Kenton found among the letters of his last mail one which he easily knew to be from his sister Lottie, by the tightly curled-up handwriting, and by the unliterary look of the slanted and huddled address of the envelope: The only doubt he could have felt in opening it was from the unwonted length at which she had written him; Lottie usually practised a laconic brevity in her notes, which were suited to the poverty of her written vocabulary rather than the affluence of her spoken word.

"Dear Dick" [her letter ran, tripping and stumbling in its course], "I have got to tell you about something that has just happened here, and you needent laugh at the speling, or the way I tell it, but just pay attention to the thing itself, if you please. That disgusting Bittridge has been here with his horrid wiggy old mother, and momma let him take Ellen to the theatre. On the way home he tried to make her promise she would marry him and at the door he kissed her. They had an awful night with her hiseterics, and I heard momma going in and out, and trying to comfort her till daylight, nearly. In the morning I went down with poppy and Boyne to breakfast, and after I came up, father went to the reading-room to get a paper, and that Bittridge was there waiting for him, and wanted to speak with him about Ellen. Poppa wouldent say a word to him, and he kept following poppa up, to make him. Boyne says be wouldent take no for an ansir, and hung on and hungon, till poppa threatened to hitt

him with his cane. Then he saw it was no use, and he
took his hand and rubbed it in poppa's face, and Boyne
believes he was trying to pull poppa's nose. Boyne acted
like I would have done; he pounded Bittridge in the back;
but of course Bittridge was too strong for him, and threw
him on the floor, and Boyne scraped his knee so that it
bledd. Then the porters came up, and caught Bittridge,
and wanted to send for a policeman, but father wouldent
let them, and the porters took Bittridge to the desk and
the clerk told him to get out instantly and they left as
soon as old Wiggy could get her things on. I don't know
where they went, but he told poppa they were going
home to-day any way. Now, Dick, I don't know what you
will want to do, and I am not going to put you up to
anything, but I know what I would do, pretty well, the
first time Bittridge showed himself in Tuskingum. You
can do just as you please, and I don't ask you to believe
me if you're think I'm so exciteable that I cant tell the
truth. I guess Boyne will say the same. Much love to
Mary. Your affectionate sister,

"Lottie.

"P. S. - Every word Lottie says is true, but I am not sure
he meant to pull his nose. The reason why he threw me
down so easily is, I have grown about a foot, and I have
not got up my strength. BOYNE.

"This is strictly confidential. They don't know we are
writing. LATTIE."

After reading this letter, Richard Kenton tore it into small
pieces, so that there should not be even so much witness as it
bore to facts that seemed to fill him with fury to the throat.
His fury was, in agreement with his temperament, the white
kind and cold kind. He was able to keep it to himself for that
reason; at supper his wife knew merely that he had something
on his mind that he did not wish to talk of; and experience had
taught her that it would be useless to try making him speak.

William Dean Howells

He slept upon his wrath, and in the morning early, at an hour when he knew there would be no loafers in the place, he went to an out-dated saddler's shop, and asked the owner, a veteran of his father's regiment, "Welks, do you happen to have a cowhide among your antiquities?"

"Regular old style?" Welks returned. "Kind they make out of a cow's hide and use on a man's?"

"Something of that sort," said Richard, with a slight smile.

The saddler said nothing more, but rummaged among the riff-raff on an upper shelf. He got down with the tapering, translucent, wicked-looking thing in his hand. "I reckon that's what you're after, squire."

"Reckon it is, Welks," said Richard, drawing it through his tubed left hand. Then he buttoned it under his coat, and paid the quarter which Welks said had always been the price of a cowhide even since he could remember, and walked away towards the station.

"How's the old colonel" Welks called after him, having forgotten to ask before.

"The colonel's all right," Richard called back, without looking round.

He walked up and down in front of the station. A local train came in from Ballardsville at 8.15, and waited for the New York special, and then returned to Ballardsville. Richard had bought a ticket for that station, and was going to take the train back, but among the passengers who descended from it when it drew in was one who saved him the trouble of going.

Bittridge, with his overcoat hanging on his arm, advanced towards him with the rest, and continued to advance, in a sort of fascination, after his neighbors, with the instinct that something was about to happen, parted on either side of

Richard, and left the two men confronted. Richard did not speak, but deliberately reached out his left hand, which he caught securely into Bittridge's collar; then he began to beat him with the cowhide wherever he could strike his writhing and twisting shape. Neither uttered a word, and except for the whir of the cowhide in the air, and the rasping sound of its arrest upon the body of Bittridge, the thing was done in perfect silence. The witnesses stood well back in a daze, from which they recovered when Richard released Bittridge with a twist of the hand that tore his collar loose and left his cravat dangling, and tossed the frayed cowhide away, and turned and walked homeward. Then one of them picked up Bittridge's hat and set it aslant on his head, and others helped pull his collar together and tie his cravat.

For the few moments that Richard Kenton remained in sight they scarcely found words coherent enough for question, and when they did, Bittridge had nothing but confused answers to give to the effect that he did not know what it meant, but he would find out. He got into a hack and had himself driven to his hotel, but he never made the inquiry which he threatened.

In his own house Richard Kenton lay down awhile, deadly sick, and his wife had to bring him brandy before he could control his nerves sufficiently to speak. Then he told her what he had done, and why, and Mary pulled off his shoes and put a hot-water bottle to his cold feet. It was not exactly the treatment for a champion, but Mary Kenton was not thinking of that, and when Richard said he still felt a little sick at the stomach she wanted him to try a drop of camphor in addition to the brandy. She said he must not talk, but she wished him so much to talk that she was glad when he began.

"It seemed to be something I had to do, Mary, but I would give anything if I had not been obliged to do it:

"Yes, I know just how you feel, Dick, and I think it's pretty hard this has come on you. I do think Ellen might -"

William Dean Howells

"It wasn't her fault, Mary. You mustn't blame her. She's had more to bear than all the rest of us." Mary looked stubbornly unconvinced, and she was not moved, apparently, by what he went on to say. "The thing now is to keep what I've done from making more mischief for her."

"What do you mean, Dick? You don't believe he'll do anything about it, do you?"

"No, I'm not afraid of that. His mouth is shut. But you can't tell how Ellen will take it. She may side with him now."

"Dick! If I thought Ellen Kenton could be such a fool as that!"

"If she's in love with him she'll take his part."

"But she can't be in love with him when she knows how he acted to your father!"

"We can't be sure of that. I know how he acted to father; but at this minute I pity him so that I could take his part against father. And I can understand how Ellen - Anyway, I must make a clean breast of it. What day is this Thursday? And they sail Saturday! I must write -"

He lifted himself on his elbow, and made as if to throw off the shawl she had spread upon him.

"No, no! I will write, Dick! I will write to your mother. What shall I say?" She whirled about, and got the paper and ink out of her writing-desk, and sat down near him to keep him from getting up, and wrote the date, and the address, "Dear Mother Kenton," which was the way she always began her letters to Mrs. Kenton, in order to distinguish her from her own mother. "Now what shall I say?"

"Simply this," answered Richard. "That I knew of what had happened in New York, and when I met him this morning I cowhided him. Ugh!"

"Well, that won't do, Dick. You've got to tell all about it. Your mother won't understand."

"Then you write what you please, and read it to me. It makes me sick to think of it." Richard closed his eyes, and Mary wrote:

"DEAR MOTHER KENTON, - I am sitting by Richard, writing at his request, about what he has done. He received a letter from New York telling him of the Bittridges' performances there, and how that wretch had insulted and abused you all. He bought a cowhide; meaning to go over to Ballardsville, and use it on him there, but B. came over on the Accommodation this morning, and Richard met him at the station. He did not attempt to resist, for Richard took him quite by surprise. Now, Mother Kenton, you know that Richard doesn't approve of violence, and the dear, sweet soul is perfectly broken-down by what he had to do. But he had to do it, and he wishes you to know at, once that he did it. He dreads the effect upon Ellen, and we must leave it to your judgment about telling her. Of course, sooner or later she must find it out. You need not be alarmed about Richard. He is just nauseated a little, and he will be all right as soon as his stomach is settled. He thinks you ought to have this letter before you sail, and with affectionate good-byes to all, in which Dick joins,

"Your loving daughter,

"Mary KENTON."

"There! Will that do?"

"Yes, that is everything that can be said," answered Richard, and Mary kissed him gratefully before sealing her letter.

"I will put a special delivery on it," she said, and her precaution availed to have the letter delivered to Mrs. Kenton the evening the family left the hotel, when it was too late to make any change in their plans, but in time to give her a bad night on the steamer, in her doubt whether she ought to let the family go, with this trouble behind them.

But she would have had a bad night on the steamer in any case, with the heat, and noise, and smell of the docks; and the steamer sailed with her at six o'clock the next morning with the doubt still open in her mind. The judge had not been of the least use to her in helping solve it, and she had not been able to bring herself to attack Lottie for writing to Richard. She knew it was Lottie who had made the mischief, but she could not be sure that it was mischief till she knew its effect upon Ellen. The girl had been carried in the arms of one of the stewards from the carriage to her berth in Lottie's room, and there she had lain through the night, speechless and sleepless.

IX

Ellen did not move or manifest any consciousness when the steamer left her dock and moved out into the stream, or take any note of the tumult that always attends a great liner's departure. At breakfast-time her mother came to her from one of the brief absences she made, in the hope that at each turn she should find her in a different mood, and asked if she would not have something to eat.

"I'm not hungry," she answered. "When will it sail?"

"Why, Ellen! We sailed two hours ago, and the pilot has just left us."

Ellen lifted herself on her elbow and stared at her. "And you let me!" she said, cruelly.

"Ellen! I will not have this!" cried her mother, frantic at the reproach. "What do you mean by my letting you? You knew that we were going to sail, didn't you? What else did you suppose we had come to the steamer for?"

"I supposed you would let me stay, if I wanted to: But go away, momma, go away! You're all against me - you, and poppa, and Lottie, and Boyne. Oh, dear! oh, dear!" She threw herself down in her berth and covered her face with the sheet, sobbing, while her mother stood by in an anguish of pity and anger. She wanted to beat the girl, she wanted to throw herself upon her, and weep with her in the misery which she shared with her.

Lottie came to the door of the state-room with an arm-load of long-stemmed roses, the gift of the young Mr. Plumpton, who had not had so much to be entreated to come down to the steamer and see her off as Boyne had pretended. "Momma," she said, "I have got to leave these roses in here, whether Ellen likes it or not. Boyne won't have them in his room, because he says the man that's with him would have a right to object; and this is half my room, anyway."

Mrs. Kenton frowned and shook her head, but Ellen answered from under the sheet, "I don't mind the roses, Lottie. I wish you'd stay with me a little while."

Lottie hesitated, having in mind the breakfast for which the horn had just sounded. But apparently she felt that one good turn deserved another, and she answered: "All right; I will, Nell. Momma, you tell Boyne to hurry, and come to Ellen as soon as he's done, and then I will go. Don't let anybody take my place."

"I wish," said Ellen, still from under the sheet, "that momma would have your breakfast sent here. I don't want Boyne."

Women apparently do not require any explanation of these swift vicissitudes in one another, each knowing probably in herself the nerves from which they proceed. Mrs. Kenton promptly assented, in spite of the sulky reluctance which Lottie's blue eyes looked at her; she motioned her violently to silence, and said: "Yes, I will, Ellen. I will send breakfast for both of you."

When she was gone, Ellen uncovered her face and asked Lottie to dip a towel in water and give it to her. As she bathed her eyes she said, "You don't care, do you, Lottie?"

"Not very much," said Lottie, unsparingly. "I can go to lunch, I suppose."

"Maybe I'll go to lunch with you," Ellen suggested, as if she were speaking of some one else.

Lottie wasted neither sympathy nor surprise on the question. "Well, maybe that would be the best thing. Why don't you come to breakfast?"

"No, I won't go to breakfast. But you go."

When Lottie joined her family in the dining-saloon she carelessly explained that Ellen had said she wanted to be alone. Before the young man, who was the only other person besides the Kentons at their table, her mother could not question her with any hope that the bad would not be made worse, and so she remained silent. Judge Kenton sat with his eyes fixed on his plate, where as yet the steward had put no breakfast for him; Boyne was supporting the dignity of the family in one of those moments of majesty from which he was so apt to lapse into childish dependence. Lottie offered him another alternative by absently laying hold of his napkin on the table.

"That's mine," he said, with husky gloom.

She tossed it back to him with prompt disdain and a deeply eye-lashed glance at a napkin on her right. The young man who sat next it said, with a smile, "Perhaps that's yours-unless I've taken my neighbor's."

Lottie gave him a stare, and when she had sufficiently punished him for his temerity said, rather sweetly, "Oh, thank you," and took the napkin.

"I hope we shall all have use for them before long," the young man ventured again.

"Well, I should think as much," returned the girl, and this was the beginning of a conversation which the young man shared successively with the judge and Mrs. Kenton as opportunity offered. He gave the judge his card across the table, and when the judge had read on it, "Rev. Hugh Breckon," he said that his name was Kenton, and he introduced the young man formally to his family. Mr. Breckon had a clean-shaven face, with an habitual smile curving into the cheeks from under a long, straight nose; his chin had a slight whopper-jaw twist that was charming; his gay eyes were blue, and a full vein came down his forehead between them from his smooth hair. When he laughed, which was often, his color brightened.

Boyne was named last, and then Mr. Breckon said, with a smile that showed all his white teeth, "Oh yes, Mr. Boyne and I are friends already - ever since we found ourselves room-mates," and but for us, as Lottie afterwards noted, they might never have known Boyne was rooming with him, and could easily have made all sorts of insulting remarks about Mr. Breckon in their ignorance.

The possibility seemed to delight Mr. Breckon; he invited her to make all the insulting remarks she could think of, any way, and professed himself a loser, so far as her real opinion was withheld from him by reason of his rashness in giving the facts away. In the electrical progress of their acquaintance she had begun walking up and down the promenade with him after they came up from breakfast; her mother had gone to Ellen; the judge had been made comfortable in his steamer-chair, and Boyne had been sent about his business.

"I will try to think some up," she promised him, "as soon as I HAVE any real opinion of you," and he asked her if he might consider that a beginning.

She looked at him out of her indomitable blue eyes, and said, "If it hadn't been for your card, and the Reverend on it, I should have said you were an actor."

"Well, well," said Mr. Breckon, with a laugh, "perhaps I am, in a way. I oughtn't to be, of course, but if a minister ever forces himself, I suppose he's acting."

"I don't see," said Lottie, instantly availing herself of the opening, "how you can get up and pray, Sunday after Sunday, whether you feel like it or not."

The young man said, with another laugh, but not so gay, "Well, the case has its difficulties."

"Or perhaps you just read prayers," Lottie sharply conjectured.

"No," he returned, "I haven't that advantage - if you think it one. I'm a sort of a Unitarian. Very advanced, too, I'm afraid."

"Is that a kind of Universalist?"

"Not - not exactly. There's an old joke - I'm not sure it's very good - which distinguishes between the sects. It's said that the Universalists think God is too good to damn them, and the Unitarians think they are too good to be damned." Lottie shrank a little from him. "Ah!" he cried, "you think it sounds wicked. Well, I'm sorry. I'm not clerical enough to joke about serious things."

He looked into her face with a pretended anxiety. "Oh, I don't know," she said, with a little scorn. "I guess if you can stand it, I can."

"I'm not sure that I can. I'm afraid it's more in keeping with an actor's profession than my own. Why," he added, as if to make a diversion, "should you have thought I was an actor?"

"I suppose because you were clean-shaved; and your pronunciation. So Englishy."

"Is it? Perhaps I ought to be proud. But I'm not an Englishman. I am a plain republican American. May I ask if you are English?"

"Oh!" said Lottie. "As if you thought such a thing. We're from Ohio."

Mr. Breckon said, "Ah!" Lottie could not make out in just what sense.

By this time they were leaning on the rail of the promenade, looking over at what little was left of Long Island, and she said, abruptly: "I think I will go and see how my father is getting along."

"Oh, do take me with you, Miss Kenton!" Mr. Breckon entreated. "I am feeling very badly about that poor old joke. I know you don't think well of me for it, and I wish to report what I've been saying to your father, and let him judge me. I've heard that it's hard to live up to Ohio people when you're at your best, and I do hope you'll believe I have not been quite at my best. Will you let me come with you?"

Lottie did not know whether he was making fun of her or not, but she said, "Oh, it's a free country," and allowed him to go with her.

His preface made the judge look rather grave; but when he came to the joke, Kenton laughed and said it was not bad.

"Oh, but that isn't quite the point," said Mr. Breckon. "The question is whether I am good in repeating it to a young lady who was seeking serious instruction on a point of theology."

"I don't know what she would have done with the instruction if she had got it," said the judge, dryly, and the young man ventured in her behalf:

"It would be difficult for any one to manage, perhaps."

"Perhaps," Kenton assented, and Lottie could see that he was thinking Ellen would know what to do with it.

She resented that, and she was in the offence that girls feel when their elders make them the subject of comment with their contemporaries. "Well, I'll leave you to discuss it alone.

I'm going to Ellen," she said, the young man vainly following her a few paces, with apologetic gurgles of laughter.

"That's right," her father consented, and then he seized the opening to speak about Ellen. "My eldest daughter is something of an invalid, but I hope we shall have her on deck before the voyage is over. She is more interested in those matters than her sister."

"Oh!" Mr. Breckon interpolated, in a note of sympathetic interest. He could not well do more.

It was enough for Judge Kenton, who launched himself upon the celebration of Ellen's gifts and qualities with a simple-hearted eagerness which he afterwards denied when his wife accused him of it, but justified as wholly safe in view of Mr. Breckon's calling and his obvious delicacy of mind. It was something that such a person would understand, and Kenton was sure that he had not unduly praised the girl. A less besotted parent might have suspected that he had not deeply interested his listener, who seemed glad of the diversion operated by Boyne's coming to growl upon his father, "Mother's bringing Ellen up."

"Oh, then, I mustn't keep your chair," said the minister, and he rose promptly from the place he had taken beside the judge, and got himself away to the other side of the ship before the judge could frame a fitting request for him to stay.

"If you had," Mrs. Kenton declared, when he regretted this to her, "I don't know what I would have done. It's bad enough for him to hear you bragging about the child without being kept to help take care of her, or keep her amused, as you call it. I will see that Ellen is kept amused without calling upon strangers." She intimated that if Kenton did not act with more self-restraint she should do little less than take Ellen ashore, and abandon him to the voyage alone. Under the intimidation he promised not to speak of Ellen again.

At luncheon, where Mr. Breckon again devoted himself to Lottie, he and Ellen vied in ignoring each other after their introduction, as far as words went. The girl smiled once or twice at what he was saying to her sister, and his glance kindled when it detected her smile. He might be supposed to spare her his conversation in her own interest, she looked so little able to cope with the exigencies of the talk he kept going.

When he addressed her she answered as if she had not been listening, and he turned back to Lottie. After luncheon he walked with her, and their acquaintance made such a swift advance that she was able to ask him if he laughed that way with everybody.

He laughed, and then he begged her pardon if he had been rude.

"Well, I don't see what there is to laugh at so much. When you ask me a thing I tell you just what I think, and it seems to set you off in a perfect gale. Don't you expect people to say what they think?"

"I think it's beautiful," said the young man, going into the gale, "and I've got to expecting it of you, at any rate. But - but it's always so surprising! It isn't what you expect of people generally, is it?"

"I don't expect it of you," said Lottie.

"No?" asked Mr. Breckon, in another gale. "Am I so uncandid?"

"I don't know about uncandid. But I should say you were slippery."

At this extraordinary criticism the young man looked graver than he had yet been able to do since the beginning of their acquaintance. He said, presently, "I wish you would explain what you mean by slippery."

"You're as close as a trap!"

"Really?"

"It makes me tired."

"If you're not too tired now I wish you would say how."

"Oh, you understand well enough. You've got me to say what I think about all sorts of things, and you haven't expressed your opinion on a single, solitary point?"

Lottie looked fiercely out to sea, turning her face so as to keep him from peering around into it in the way he had. For that reason, perhaps, he did not try to do so. He answered, seriously: "I believe you are partly right. I'm afraid I haven't seemed quite fair. Couldn't you attribute my closeness to something besides my slipperiness?" He began to laugh again. "Can't you imagine my being interested in your opinions so much more than my own that I didn't care to express mine?"

Lottie said, impatiently, "Oh, pshaw!" She had hesitated whether to say, "Rats!"

"But now," he pursued, "if you will suggest some point on which I can give you an opinion, I promise solemnly to do so," but he was not very solemn as he spoke.

"Well, then, I will," she said. "Don't you think it's very strange, to say the least, for a minister to be always laughing so much?"

Mr. Breckon gave a peal of delight, and answered, "Yes, I certainly do." He controlled himself so far as to say: "Now I think I've been pretty open with you, and I wish you'd answer me a question. Will you?"

"Well, I will - one," said Lottie.

"It may be two or three; but I'll begin with one. Why do you think a minister ought to be more serious than other men?"

"Why? Well, I should think you'd know. You wouldn't laugh at a funeral, would you?"

"I've been at some funerals where it would have been a relief to laugh, and I've wanted to cry at some weddings. But you think it wouldn't do?"

"Of course it wouldn't. I should think you'd know as much as that," said Lottie, out of patience with him.

"But a minister isn't always marrying or burying people; and in the intervals, why shouldn't he be setting them an example of harmless cheerfulness?"

"He ought to be thinking more about the other world, I should say."

"Well, if he believes there is another world -"

"Why! Don't you?" she broke out on him.

Mr. Breckon ruled himself and continued - "as strenuously and unquestionably as he ought, he has greater reason than other men for gayety through his faith in a happier state of being than this. That's one of the reasons I use against myself when I think of leaving off laughing. Now, Miss Kenton," he concluded, "for such a close and slippery nature, I think I've been pretty frank," and he looked round and down into her face with a burst of laughter that could be heard an the other side of the ship. He refused to take up any serious topic after that, and he returned to his former amusement of making her give herself away.

That night Lottie came to her room with an expression so decisive in her face that Ellen, following it with vague, dark eyes as it showed itself in the glass at which her sister stood taking out the first dismantling hairpins before going to bed, could not fail of something portentous in it.

"Well," said Lottie, with severe finality, "I haven't got any use for THAT young man from this time out. Of all the tiresome people, he certainly takes the cake. You can have him, Ellen, if you want him."

"What's the matter with him?" asked Ellen, with a voice in sympathy with the slow movement of her large eyes as she lay in her berth, staring at Lottie.

"There's everything the matter, that oughtn't to be. He's too trivial for anything: I like a man that's serious about one thing in the universe, at least, and that's just what Mr. Breckon isn't." She went at such length into his disabilities that by the time she returned to the climax with which she started she was ready to clamber into the upper berth; and as she snapped the electric button at its head she repeated, "He's trivial."

"Isn't it getting rough?" asked Ellen. "The ship seems to be tipping."

"Yes, it is," said Lottie, crossly. "Good-night."

If the Rev. Mr. Breckon was making an early breakfast in the hope of sooner meeting Lottie, who had dismissed him the night before without encouraging him to believe that she wished ever to see him again, he was destined to disappointment. The deputation sent to breakfast by the paradoxical family whose acquaintance he had made on terms of each forbidding intimacy, did not include the girl who had frankly provoked his confidence and severely snubbed it. He had left her brother very sea-sick in their state-room, and her mother was reported by her father to be feeling the motion too much to venture out. The judge was, in fact, the only person at table when Breckon sat down; but when he had accounted for his wife's absence, and confessed that he did not believe either of his daughters was coming, Ellen gainsaid him by appearing and advancing quite steadily along the saloon to the place beside him. It had not gone so far as this in the judge's experience of a neurotic invalid without his learning to ask her no questions about herself. He had always a hard task in refraining, but he had grown able to refrain, and now he merely looked unobtrusively glad to see her, and asked her where Lottie was.

"Oh, she doesn't want any breakfast, she says. Is momma sick, too? Where's Boyne?"

The judge reported as to her mother, and Mr. Breckon, after the exchange of a silent salutation with the girl, had a gleeful moment in describing Boyne's revolt at the steward's notion of gruel. "I'm glad to see you so well, Miss Kenton," he concluded.

"I suppose I will be sick, too, if it gets rougher," she said, and she turned from him to give a rather compendious order to the table steward.

"Well, you've got an appetite, Ellen," her father ventured.

"I don't believe I will eat anything," she checked him, with a falling face.

Breckon came to the aid of the judge. "If you're not sick now, I prophesy you won't be, Miss Kenton. It can't get much rougher, without doing something uncommon."

"Is it a storm?" she asked, indifferently.

"It's what they call half a gale, I believe. I don't know how they measure it."

She smiled warily in response to his laugh, and said to her father, "Are you going up after breakfast, poppa?"

"Why, if you want to go, Ellen -"

"Oh, I wasn't asking for that; I am going back to Lottie. But I should think you would like the air. Won't it do you good?"

"I'm all right," said the judge, cheered by her show of concern for some one else. "I suppose it's rather wet on deck?" he referred himself to Breckon.

"Well, not very, if you keep to the leeward. She doesn't seem a very wet boat."

"What is a wet boat" Ellen asked, without lifting her sad eyes.

"Well, really, I'm afraid it's largely a superstition. Passengers like to believe that some boats are less liable to ship seas - to run into waves - than others; but I fancy that's to give themselves the air of old travellers."

She let the matter lapse so entirely that he supposed she had forgotten it in all its bearings, when she asked, "Have you been across many times?"

"Not many-four or five."

"This is our first time," she volunteered.

"I hope it won't be your last. I know you will enjoy it." She fell listless again, and Breckon imagined he had made a break. "Not," he added, with an endeavor for lightness, "that I suppose you're going for pleasure altogether. Women, now-adays, are above that, I understand. They go abroad for art's sake, and to study political economy, and history, and literature -"

"My daughter," the judge interposed, "will not do much in that way, I hope."

The girl bent her head over her plate and frowned.

"Oh, then," said Breckon, "I will believe that she's going for purely selfish enjoyment. I should like to be justified in making that my object by a good example."

Ellen looked up and gave him a look that cut him short in his glad note. The lifting of her eyelids was like the rise of the curtain upon some scene of tragedy which was all the more impressive because it seemed somehow mixed with shame. This poor girl, whom he had pitied as an invalid, was a sufferer from some spiritual blight more pathetic than broken health. He pulled his mind away from the conjecture that tempted it and went on: "One of the advantages of going over the fourth or fifth time is that you're relieved from a discoverer's duties to Europe. I've got absolutely nothing before me now, but at first I had to examine every object of interest on the Continent, and form an opinion about thousands of objects that had no interest for me. I hope Miss Kenton will take warning from me."

He had not addressed Ellen directly, and her father answered: "We have no definite plans as yet, but we don't mean to over-work ourselves even if we've come for a rest. I don't know," he added, "but we had better spend our summer in England. It's easier getting about where you know the language."

The judge seemed to refer his ideas to Breckon for criticism, and the young man felt authorized to say, "Oh, so many of them know the language everywhere now, that it's easy getting about in any country."

"Yes, I suppose so," the judge vaguely deferred.

"Which," Ellen demanded of the young man with a nervous suddenness, "do you think is the most interesting country?"

He found himself answering with equal promptness, "Oh, Italy, of course."

"Can we go to Italy, poppa?" asked the girl.

"I shouldn't advise you to go there at once" Breckon intervened, smiling. "You'd find it Pretty hot there now. Florence, or Rome, or Naples - you can't think of them."

"We have it pretty hot in Central Ohio," said the judge, with latent pride in his home climate, "What sort of place is Holland?"

"Oh, delightful! And the boat goes right on to Rotterdam, you know."

"Yes. We had arranged to leave it at Boulogne," but we could change. "Do you think your mother would like Holland?" The judge turned to his daughter.

"I think she would like Italy better. She's read more about it," said the girl.

"Rise of the Dutch Republic," her father suggested.

"Yes, I know. But she's read more about Italy!"

"Oh, well," Breckon yielded, "the Italian lakes wouldn't be impossible. And you might find Venice fairly comfortable."

"We could go to Italy, then," said the judge to his daughter, "if your mother prefers."

Breckon found the simplicity of this charming, and he tasted a yet finer pleasure in the duplicity; for he divined that the father was seeking only to let his daughter have her way in pretending to yield to her mother's preference.

It was plain that the family's life centred, as it ought, about this sad, sick girl, the heart of whose mystery he perceived, on reflection, he had not the wish to pluck out. He might come to know it, but he would not try to know it; if it offered itself he might even try not to know it. He had sometimes found it more helpful with trouble to be ignorant of its cause.

In the mean time he had seen that these Kentons were sweet, good people, as he phrased their quality to himself. He had come to terms of impersonal confidence the night before with Boyne, who had consulted him upon many more problems and predicaments of life than could have yet beset any boy's experience, probably with the wish to make provision for any possible contingency of the future. The admirable principles which Boyne evolved for his guidance from their conversation were formulated with a gravity which Breckon could outwardly respect only by stifling his laughter in his pillow. He rather liked the way Lottie had tried to weigh him in her balance and found him, as it were, of an imponderable levity. With his sense of being really very light at most times, and with most people, he was aware of having been particularly light with Lottie, of having been slippery, of having, so far as responding to her frankness was concerned, been close. He relished the unsparing honesty with which she had denounced him, and though he did not yet know his outcast condition with relation to her, he could not think of her without a smile of wholly disinterested liking. He did not know, as a man of earlier date would have known, all that the little button in the judge's lapel meant; but he knew that it meant service in the civil war, a struggle which he vaguely and impersonally revered, though its details were of much the same dimness for him as those of the Revolution and the War of 1812. The modest distrust which had grown upon the bold self-confidence of Kenton's earlier manhood could not have been more tenderly and reverently imagined; and Breckon's conjecture of things suffered for love's sake against sense and conviction in him were his further tribute to a character which existed, of course, mainly in this conjecture. It appeared to him that Kenton was held not only in the subjection to his wife's, judgment, which befalls, and doubtless becomes, a man after many years of marriage, but that he was in the actual performance of more than common renunciation of his judgment in deference to the good woman. She in turn, to be sure, offered herself a sacrifice to the whims of the sick girl, whose worst whim was having no wish that could be ascertained, and who now, after two days of her mother's devotion, was cast upon her own resources by the inconstant barometer. It had become apparent that Miss Kenton was her father's favorite in a special sense, and that his partial affection for her was of much older date than her mother's. Not less charming than her fondness for her father was the openness with which she disabled his wisdom because of his partiality to her.

X

When they left the breakfast table the first morning of the rough weather, Breckon offered to go on deck with Miss Kenton, and put her where she could see the waves. That had been her shapeless ambition, dreamily expressed with reference to some time, as they rose. Breckon asked, "Why not now?" and he promised to place her chair on deck where she could enjoy the spectacle safe from any seas the boat might ship. Then she recoiled, and she recoiled the further upon her father's urgence. At the foot of the gangway she looked wistfully up the reeling stairs, and said that she saw her shawl and Lottie's among the others solemnly swaying from the top railing. "Oh, then," Breckon pressed her, "you could be made comfortable without the least trouble."

"I ought to go and see how Lottie is getting along," she murmured.

Her father said he would see for her, and on this she explicitly renounced her ambition of going up. "You couldn't do anything," she said, coldly.

"If Miss Lottie is very sea-sick she's beyond all earthly aid," Breckon ventured. "She'd better be left to the vain ministrations of the stewardess."

Ellen looked at him in apparent distrust of his piety, if not of his wisdom. "I don't believe I could get up the stairs," she said.

"Well," he admitted, "they're not as steady as land - going stairs." Her father discreetly kept silence, and, as no one offered to help her, she began to climb the crazy steps, with Breckon close behind her in latent readiness for her fall.

From the top she called down to the judge, "Tell momma I will only stay a minute." But later, tucked into her chair on the lee of the bulkhead, with Breckon bracing himself against it beside her, she showed no impatience to return. "Are they never higher than that" she required of him, with her wan eyes critically on the infinite procession of the surges.

"They must be," Breckon answered, "if there's any truth in common report. I've heard of their running mountains high. Perhaps they used rather low mountains to measure them by. Or the measurements may not have been very exact. But common report never leaves much to the imagination."

"That was the way at Niagara," the girl assented; and Breckon obligingly regretted that he had never been there. He thought it in good taste that she should not tell him he ought to go. She merely said, "I was there once with poppa," and did not press her advantage. "Do they think," she asked, "that it's going to be a very long voyage?"

"I haven't been to the smoking-room - that's where most of the thinking is done on such points; the ship's officers never seem to know about it - since the weather changed. Should you mind it greatly?"

"I wouldn't care if it never ended," said the girl, with such a note of dire sincerity that Breckon instantly changed his first mind as to her words implying a pose. She took any deeper implication from them in adding, "I didn't know I should like being at sea."

"Well, if you're not sea-sick," he assented, "there are not many pleasanter things in life."

She suggested, "I suppose I'm not well enough to be sea-sick."
Then she seemed to become aware of something provisional in
his attendance, and she said, "You mustn't stay on my account.
I can get down when I want to."

"Do let me stay," he entreated, "unless you'd really rather not,"
and as there was no chair immediately attainable, he crouched
on the deck beside hers.

"It makes me think," she said, and he perceived that she meant
the sea, "of the cold-white, heavy plunging foam in 'The
Dream of Fair Women.' The words always seemed drenched!"

"Ah, Tennyson, yes," said Breckon, with a disposition to smile
at the simple-heartedness of the literary allusion. "Do young
ladies read poetry much in Ohio?"

"I don't believe they do," she answered. "Do they anywhere?"

"That's one of the things I should like to know. Is Tennyson
your favorite poet?"

"I don't believe I have any," said Ellen. "I used to like
Whither, and Emerson; aid Longfellow, too."

"Used to! Don't you now?"

"I don't read them so much now," and she made a pause,
behind which he fancied her secret lurked. But he shrank from
knowing it if he might.

"You're all great readers in your family," he suggested, as a
polite diversion.

"Lottie isn't," she answered, dreamily. "She hates it."

"Ah, I referred more particularly to the others," said Breckon,
and he began to laugh, and then checked himself. "Your
mother, and the judge - and your brother -"

"Boyne reads about insects," she admitted.

"He told me of his collection of cocoons. He seems to be afraid it has suffered in his absence."

"I'm afraid it has," said Ellen, and then remained silent.

"There!" the young man broke out, pointing seaward. "That's rather a fine one. Doesn't that realize your idea of something mountains high? Unless your mountains are very high in Ohio!"

"It is grand. And the gulf between! But we haven't any in our part. It's all level. Do you believe the tenth wave is larger than the rest?"

"Why, the difficulty is to know which the tenth wave is, or when to begin counting."

"Yes," said the girl, and she added, vaguely: "I suppose it's like everything else in that. We have to make-believe before we can believe anything."

"Something like an hypothesis certainly seems necessary," Breckon assented, with a smile for the gravity of their discourse. "We shouldn't have the atomic theory without it." She did not say anything, and he decided that the atomic theory was beyond the range of her reading. He tried to be more concrete. "We have to make-believe in ourselves before we can believe, don't we? And then we sometimes find we are wrong!" He laughed, but she asked, with tragical seriousness:

"And what ought you to do when you find out you are mistaken in yourself?"

"That's what I'm trying to decide," he replied. "Sometimes I feel like renouncing myself altogether; but usually I give myself another chance. I dare say if I hadn't been so forbearing I might have agreed with your sister about my unfitness for the ministry."

"With Lottie?"

"She thinks I laugh too much!"

"I don't see why a minister shouldn't laugh if he feels like it.
And if there's something to laugh at."

"Ah, that's just the point! Is there ever anything to laugh at? If
we looked closely enough at things, oughtn't we rather to cry?"
He laughed in retreat from the serious proposition. "But it
wouldn't do to try making each other cry instead of laugh,
would it? I suppose your sister would rather have me cry."

"I don't believe Lottie thought much about it," said Ellen; and
at this point Mr. Breckon yielded to an impulse.

"I should think I had really been of some use if I had made you
laugh, Miss Kenton."

"Me?"

"You look as if you laughed with your whole heart when you
did laugh."

She glanced about, and Breckon decided that she had found
him too personal. "I wonder if I could walk, with the ship
tipping so?" she asked.

"Well, not far," said Breckon, with a provisional smile, and
then he was frightened from his irony by her flinging aside her
wraps and starting to her feet. Before he could scramble to his
own, she had slid down the reeling promenade half to the
guard, over which she seemed about to plunge. He hurled
himself after her; he could not have done otherwise; and it was
as much in a wild clutch for support as in a purpose to save her
that he caught her in his arms and braced himself against the
ship's slant. "Where are you going? What are you trying to

do?" he shouted.

"I wanted to go down-stairs," she protested, clinging to him.

"You were nearer going overboard," he retorted. "You shouldn't have tried." He had not fully formulated his reproach when the ship righted herself with a counter-roll and plunge, and they were swung staggering back together against the bulkhead. The door of the gangway was within reach, and Breckon laid hold of the rail beside it and put the girl within. "Are you hurt?" he asked.

"No, no; I'm not hurt," she panted, sinking on the cushioned benching where usually rows of semi-sea-sick people were lying.

"I thought you might have been bruised against the bulkhead," he said. "Are you sure you're not hurt that I can't get you anything? From the steward, I mean?"

"Only help me down-stairs," she answered. "I'm perfectly well," and Breckon was so willing on these terms to close the incident that he was not aware of the bruise on his own arm, which afterwards declared itself in several primitive colors. "Don't tell them," she added. "I want to come up again."

"Why, certainly not," he consented; but Boyne Kenton, who had been an involuntary witness of the fact from a point on the forward promenade, where he had stationed himself to study the habits of the stormy petrel at a moment so favorable to the acquaintance of the petrel (having left a seasick bed for the purpose), was of another mind. He had been alarmed, and, as it appeared in the private interview which he demanded of his mother, he had been scandalized.

"It is bad enough the way Lottie is always going on with fellows. And now, if Ellen is going to begin!"

"But, Boyne, child," Mrs. Kenton argued, in an equilibrium

William Dean Howells

between the wish to laugh at her son and the wish to box his ears, "how could she help his catching her if he was to save her from pitching overboard?"

"That's just it! He will always think that she did it just so he would have to catch her."

"I don't believe any one would think that of Ellen," said Mrs. Kenton, gravely.

"Momma! You don't know what these Eastern fellows are. There are so few of them that they're used to having girls throw themselves at them, and they will think anything, ministers and all. You ought to talk to Ellen, and caution her. Of course, she isn't like Lottie; but if Lottie's been behaving her way with Mr. Breckon, he must suppose the rest of the family is like her."

"Boyne," said his mother, provisionally, "what sort of person is Mr. Breckon?"

"Well, I think he's kind of frivolous."

"Do you, Boyne?"

"I don't suppose he means any harm by it, but I don't like to see a minister laugh so much. I can't hardly get him to talk seriously about anything. And I just know he makes fun of Lottie. I don't mean that he always makes fun with me. He didn't that night at the vaudeville, where I first saw him."

"What do you mean?"

"Don't you remember? I told you about it last winter."

"And was Mr. Breckon that gentleman?"

"Yes; but he didn't know who I was when we met here."

"Well, upon my word, Boyne, I think you might have told us before," said his mother, in not very definite vexation. "Go along, now!"

Boyne stood talking to his mother, with his hands, which he had not grown to, largely planted on the jambs of her state-room door. She was keeping her berth, not so much because she was sea-sick as because it was the safest place in the unsteady ship to be in. "Do you want me to send Ellen to you!"

"I will attend to Ellen, Boyne," his mother snubbed him. "How is Lottie?"

"I can't tell whether she's sick or not. I went to see about her and she motioned me away, and fairly screamed when I told her she ought to keep out in the air. Well, I must be going up again myself, or -"

Before lunch, Boyne had experienced the alternative which he did not express, although his theory and practice of keeping in the open air ought to have rendered him immune. Breckon saw his shock of hair, and his large eyes, like Ellen's in their present gloom, looking out of it on the pillow of the upper berth, when he went to their room to freshen himself for the luncheon, and found Boyne averse even to serious conversation: He went to lunch without him. None of the Kentons were at table, and he had made up his mind to lunch alone when Ellen appeared, and came wavering down the aisle to the table. He stood up to help her, but seeing how securely she stayed herself from chair to chair he sank down again.

"Poppy is sick, too, now," she replied, as if to account for being alone.

"And you're none the worse for your little promenade?" The steward came to Breckon's left shoulder with a dish, and after an effort to serve himself from it he said, with a slight gasp, "The other side, please." Ellen looked at him, but did not speak, and he made haste to say: "The doctor goes so far as to admit that its half a gale. I don't know just what measure the first officer would have for it. But I congratulate you on a very typical little storm, Miss Kenton; perfectly safe, but very decided. A great many people cross the Atlantic without anything half as satisfactory. There is either too much or too little of this sort of thing." He went on talking about the weather, and had got such a distance from the point of beginning that he had cause to repent being brought back to it when she asked:

"Did the doctor think, you were hurt?"

"Well, perhaps I ought to be more ashamed than I am," said Breckon. "But I thought I had better make sure. And it's only a bruise -"

"Won't you let ME help you!" she asked, as another dish intervened at his right. "I hurt you."

Breckon laughed at her solemn face and voice. "If you'll exonerate yourself first," he answered: "I couldn't touch a morsel that conveyed confession of the least culpability on your part. Do you consent? Otherwise, I pass this dish. And really I want some!"

"Well," she sadly consented, and he allowed her to serve his plate.

"More yet, please," he said. "A lot!"

"Is that enough?"

"Well, for the first helping. And don't offer to cut it up for me! My proud spirit draws the line at cutting up. Besides, a fork will do the work with goulash."

"Is that what it is?" she asked, but not apparently because she cared to know.

"Unless you prefer to naturalize it as stew. It seems to have come in with the Hungarian bands. I suppose you have them in -"

"Tuskingum? No, it is too small. But I heard them at a restaurant in New York where my brother took us."

"In the spirit of scientific investigation? It's strange how a common principle seems to pervade both the Hungarian music and cooking - the same wandering airs and flavors - wild, vague, lawless harmonies in both. Did you notice it?"

Ellen shook her head. The look of gloom which seemed to Breckon habitual in it came back into her face, and he had a fantastic temptation to see how far he could go with her sad consciousness before she should be aware that he was experimenting upon it. He put this temptation from him, and was in the enjoyment of a comfortable self-righteousness when it returned in twofold power upon him with the coming of some cutlets which capriciously varied the repast.

"Ah, now, Miss Kenton, if you were to take pity on my helplessness!"

"Why, certainly!" She possessed herself of his plate, and began to cut up the meat for him. "Am I making the bites too small?" she asked, with an upward glance at him.

"Well, I don't know. Should you think so?" he returned, with a smile that out-measured the morsels on the plate before her.

She met his laughing eyes with eyes that questioned his honesty, at first sadly, and then indignantly. She dropped the knife and fork upon the plate and rose.

"Oh, Miss Kenton!" he penitently entreated.

But she was down the slanting aisle and out of the reeling door before he could decide what to do.

XI

It seemed to Breckon that he had passed through one of those accessions of temperament, one of those crises of natural man, to put it in the terms of an older theology than he professed, that might justify him in recurring to his original sense of his unfitness for his sacred calling, as he would hardly ham called it: He had allowed his levity to get the better of his sympathy, and his love of teasing to overpower that love of helping which seemed to him his chief right and reason for being a minister: To play a sort of poor practical joke upon that melancholy girl (who was also so attractive) was not merely unbecoming to him as a minister; it was cruel; it was vulgar; it was ungentlemanly. He could not say less than ungentlemanly, for that seemed to give him the only pang that did him any good. Her absolute sincerity had made her such an easy prey that he ought to have shrunk from the shabby temptation in abhorrence.

It is the privilege of a woman, whether she wills it or not, to put a man who is in the wrong concerning her much further in the wrong than he could be from his offence. Breckon did not know whether he was suffering more or less because he was suffering quite hopelessly, but he was sure that he was suffering justly, and he was rather glad, if anything, that he must go on suffering. His first impulse had been to go at once to Judge Kenton and own his wrong, and take the consequences - in fact, invite them. But Breckon forbore for two reasons: one, that he had already appeared before the judge with the confession of having possibly made an unclerical joke to his younger daughter; the other, that the judge might not consider levity towards the elder so venial; and though Breckon wished to be both punished and pardoned, in the final analysis, perhaps, he most wished to be pardoned. Without pardon he could see no way to repair the wrong he had done. Perhaps he wished even to retrieve himself in the girl's eyes, or wished for the chance of trying.

Ellen went away to her state-room and sat down on the sofa opposite Lottie, and she lost herself in a muse in which she was found by the voice of the sufferer in the berth.

"If you haven't got anything better to do than come in here and stare at me, I wish you would go somewhere else and stare. I can tell you it isn't any joke."

"I didn't know I was staring at you," said Ellen, humbly.

"It would be enough to have you rising and sinking there, without your staring at all: If you're going to stay, I wish you'd lie down. I don't see why you're so well, anyway, after getting us all to come on this wild-goose chase."

"I know, I know," Ellen strickenly deprecated. "But I'm not going to stay. I jest came for my things."

"Is that giggling simpleton sick? I hope he is!"

"Mr. Breckon?" Ellen asked, though she knew whom Lottie meant. "No, he isn't sick. He was at lunch."

"Was poppa?"

"He was at breakfast."

"And momma?"

"She and Boyne are both in bed. I don't know whether they're very sick."

William Dean Howells

"Well, then, I'll just tell you what, Ellen Kenton!" Lottie sat up in accusal. "You were staring at something he said; and the first thing we all know it will be another case of Bittridge!" Ellen winced, but Lottie had no pity. "You don't know it, because you don't know anything, and I'm not blaming you; but if you let that simpleton - I don't care if he is a minister! - go 'round with you when your family are all sick abed, you'll be having the whole ship to look after you."

"Be still, Lottie!" cried Ellen. "You are awful," and, with a flaming face, she escaped from the state-room.

She did not know where else to go, and she beat along the sides of the corridor as far as the dining-saloon. She had a dim notion of trying to go up into the music-room above, but a glance at the reeling steep of the stairs forbade. With her wraps on her arm and her sea-cap in her hand, she stood clinging to the rail-post.

Breckon came out of the saloon. "Oh, Miss Kenton," he humbly entreated, "don't try to go on deck! It's rougher than ever."

"I was going to the music-room," she faltered.

"Let me help you, then," he said again. They mounted the gangway-steps, but this time with his hand under her elbow, and his arm alert as before in a suspended embrace against her falling.

She had lost the initiative of her earlier adventure; she could only submit herself to his guidance. But he almost outdid her in meekness, when he got her safely placed in a corner whence she could not be easily flung upon the floor. "You must have found it very stuffy below; but, indeed, you'd better not try going out."

"Do you think it isn't safe here?" she asked.

"Oh yes. As long as you keep quiet. May I get you something to read? They seem to have a pretty good little library."

They both glanced at the case of books; from which the steward-librarian was setting them the example of reading a volume.

"No, I don't want to read. You musn't let me keep you from it."

"Well, one can read any time. But one hasn't always the chance to say that one is ashamed. Don't pretend you don't understand, Miss Kenton! I didn't really mean anything. The temptation to let you exaggerate my disability was too much for me. Say that you despise me! It would be such a comfort."

"Weren't you hurt?"

"A little - a little more than a little, but not half so much as I deserved - not to the point of not being able to cut up my meat. Am I forgiven? I'll promise to cut up all your meat for you at dinner! Ah, I'm making it worse!"

"Oh no. Please don't speak of it"

"Could you forbid my thinking of it, too?" He did not wait for her to answer. "Then here goes! One, two, three, and the thought is banished forever. Now what shall we speak of, or think of? We finished up the weather pretty thoroughly this morning. And if you have not the weather and the ship's run when you're at sea, why, you are at sea. Don't you think it would be a good plan, when they stick those little flags into the chart, to show how far we've come in the last twenty-four hours, if they'd supply a topic for the day? They might have topics inscribed on the flags-standard topics, that would serve for any voyage. We might leave port with History - say, personal history; that would pave the way to a general acquaintance among the passengers. Then Geography, and if the world is really round, and what keeps the sea from spilling.

Then Politics, and the comparative advantages of monarchical and republican governments, for international discussion. Then Pathology, and whether you're usually sea-sick, and if there is any reliable remedy. Then - for those who are still up - Poetry and Fiction; whether women really like Kipling, and what kind of novels you prefer. There ought to be about ten topics. These boats are sometimes very slow. Can't you suggest something, Miss Kenton? There is no hurry! We've got four to talk over, for we must bring up the arrears, you know. And now we'll begin with personal history. Your sister doesn't approve of me, does she?"

"My sister?" Ellen faltered, and, between the conscience to own the fact and the kindness to deny it, she stopped altogether.

"I needn't have asked. She told me so herself, in almost as many words. She said I was slippery, and as close as a trap. Miss Kenton! I have the greatest wish to know whether I affect you as both slippery and close!"

"I don't always know what Lottie means."

"She means what she says; and I feel that I am under condemnation till I reform. I don't know how to stop being slippery, but I'm determined to stop being close. Will you tell her that for me? Will you tell her that you never met an opener, franker person? - of course, except herself! - and that so far from being light I seemed to you particularly heavy? Say that I did nothing but talk about myself, and that when you wanted to talk about yourself you couldn't get in a word edgewise. Do try, now, Miss Kenton, and see if you can! I don't want you to invent a character for me, quite."

"Why, there's nothing to say about me," she began in compliance with his gayety, and then she fell helpless from it.

"Well, then, about Tuskingum. I should like to hear about Tuskingum, so much!"

"I suppose we like it because we've always lived there. You haven't been much in the West, have you?"

"Not as much as I hope to be." He had found that Western people were sometimes sensitive concerning their section and were prepared to resent complacent ignorance of it. "I've always thought it must be very interesting."

"It isn't," said the girl. "At least, not like the East. I used to be provoked when the lecturers said anything like that; but when you've been to New York you see what they mean."

"The lecturers?" he queried.

"They always stayed at our house when they lectured in Tuskingum."

"Ah! Oh yes," said Breckon, grasping a situation of which he had heard something, chiefly satirical. "Of course. And is your father - is Judge Kenton literary? Excuse me!"

"Only in his history. He's writing the history of his regiment; or he gets the soldiers to write down all they can remember of the war, and then he puts their stories together."

"How delightful!" said Breckon. "And I suppose it's a great pleasure to him."

"I don't believe it is," said Ellen. "Poppa doesn't believe in war any more."

"Indeed!" said Breckon. "That is very interesting."

"Sometimes when I'm helping him with it -"

"Ah, I knew you must help him!"

"And he comes to a place where there has been a dreadful slaughter, it seems as if he felt worse about it than I did. He

William Dean Howells

isn't sure that it wasn't all wrong. He thinks all war is wrong now."

"Is he - has he become a follower of Tolstoy?"

"He's read him. He says he's the only man that ever gave a true account of battles; but he had thought it all out for himself before he read Tolstoy about fighting. Do you think it is right to revenge an injury?"

"Why, surely not!" said Breckon, rather startled.

"That is what we say," the girl pursued. "But if some one had injured you - abused your confidence, and - insulted you, what would you do?"

"I'm not sure that I understand," Breckon began. The inquiry was superficially impersonal, but he reflected that women are never impersonal, or the sons of women, for that matter, and he suspected an intimate ground. His suspicions were confirmed when Miss Kenton said: "It seems easy enough to forgive anything that's done to yourself; but if it's done to some one else, too, have you the right - isn't it wrong to let it go?"

"You think the question of justice might come in then? Perhaps it ought.But what is justice? And where does your duty begin to be divided?" He saw her following him with alarming intensity, and he shrank from the responsibility before him. What application might not she make of his words in the case, whatever it was, which he chose not to imagine? "To tell you the truth, Miss Kenton, I'm not very clear on that point - I'm not sure that I'm disinterested."

"Disinterested?"

"Yes; you know that I abused your confidence at luncheon; and until I know whether the wrong involved any one else -"
He looked at her with hovering laughter in his eyes which took

wing at the reproach in hers. "But if we are to be serious -"

"Oh no," she said, "it isn't a serious matter." But in the helplessness of her sincerity she could not carry it off lightly, or hide from him that she was disappointed.

He tried to make talk about other things. She responded vaguely, and when she had given herself time she said she believed she would go to Lottie; she was quite sure she could get down the stairs alone. He pursued her anxiously, politely, and at the head of her corridor took leave of her with a distinct sense of having merited his dismissal.

"I see what you mean, Lottie," she said, "about Mr. Breckon."

Lottie did not turn her head on the pillow. "Has it taken you the whole day to find it out?"

XII

The father and the mother had witnessed with tempered satisfaction the interest which seemed to be growing up between Ellen and the young minister. By this time they had learned not to expect too much of any turn she might take; she reverted to a mood as suddenly as she left it. They could not quite make out Breckon himself; he was at least as great a puzzle to them as their own child was.

"It seems," said Mrs. Kenton, in their first review of the affair, after Boyne had done a brother's duty in trying to bring Ellen under their mother's censure, "that he was the gentleman who discussed the theatre with Boyne at the vaudeville last winter. Boyne just casually mentioned it. I was so provoked!"

"I don't see what bearing the fact has," the judge remarked.

"Why, Boyne liked him very much that night, but now he seems to feel very much as Lottie does about him. He thinks he laughs too much."

"I don't know that there's much harm in that," said the judge. "And I shouldn't value Boyne's opinion of character very highly."

"I value any one's intuitions - especially children's."

"Boyne's in that middle state where he isn't quite a child. And so is Lottie, for that matter."

"That is true," their mother assented. "And we ought to be glad of anything that takes Ellen's mind off herself. If I could only believe she was forgetting that wretch!"

"Does she ever speak of him?"

"She never hints of him, even. But her mind may be full of him all the time."

The judge laughed impatiently. "It strikes me that this young Mr. Breckon hasn't much advantage of Ellen in what Lottie calls closeness!"

"Ellen has always been very reserved. It would have been better for her if she hadn't. Oh, I scarcely dare to hope anything! Rufus, I feel that in everything of this kind we are very ignorant and inexperienced."

"Inexperienced!" Renton retorted. "I don't want any more experience of the kind Ellen has given us."

"I don't mean that. I mean - this Mr. Breckon. I can't tell what attracts him in the child. She must appear very crude and uncultivated to him. You needn't resent it so! I know she's read a great deal, and you've made her think herself intellectual - but the very simple-heartedness of the way she would show out her reading would make such a young man see that she wasn't like the girls he was used to. They would hide their intellectuality, if they had any. It's no use your trying to fight it Mr. Kenton. We are country people, and he knows it."

"Tuskingum isn't country!" the judge declared.

"It isn't city. And we don't know anything about the world, any of us. Oh, I suppose we can read and write! But we don't know the a, b, c of the things he, knows. He, belongs to a kind of society - of people - in New York that I had glimpses of in the winter, but that I never imagined before. They made me feel very belated and benighted - as if I hadn't, read or thought anything. They didn't mean to; but I couldn't help it, and they couldn't."

"You - you've been frightened out of your propriety by what you've seen in New York," said her husband.

"I've been frightened, certainly. And I wish you had been, too. I wish you wouldn't be so conceited about Ellen. It scares me to see you so. Poor, sick thing, her looks are all gone! You must see that. And she doesn't dress like the girls he's used to. I know we've got her things in New York; but she doesn't wear them like a New-Yorker. I hope she isn't going in for MORE unhappiness!"

At the thought of this the judge's crest fell. "Do you believe she's getting interested in him?" he asked, humbly.

"No, no; I don't say that. But promise me you won't encourage her in it. And don't, for pity's sake, brag about her to him."

"No, I won't," said the judge, and he tacitly repented having done so.

The weather had changed, and when he went up from this interview with his wife in their stateroom he found a good many people strung convalescently along the promenade on their steamer-chairs. These, so far as they were women, were of such sick plainness that when he came to Ellen his heart throbbed with a glad resentment of her mother's aspersion of her health and beauty. She looked not only very well, and very pretty, but in a gay red cap and a trig jacket she looked, to her father's uncritical eyes, very stylish. The glow left his heart at eight of the empty seat beside her.

"Where is Lottie?" he asked, though it was not Lottie's whereabouts that interested him.

"Oh, she's walking with Mr. Breckon somewhere," said Ellen.

"Then she's made up her mind to tolerate him, has she?" the father asked, more lightly than he felt.

Ellen smiled. "That wasn't anything very serious, I guess. At any rate, she's walking with him."

"What book is that?" he asked, of the volume she was tilting back and forth under her hand.

She showed it. "One of his. He brought it up to amuse me, he said."

"While he was amusing himself with Lottie," thought the judge, in his jealousy for her. "It is going the same old way. Well!" What he said aloud was, "And is it amusing you?"

"I haven't looked at it yet," said the girl. "It's amusing enough to watch the sea. Oh, poppa! I never thought I should care so much for it."

"And you're glad we came?"

"I don't want to think about that. I just want to know that I'm here." She pressed his arm gently, significantly, where he sat provisionally in the chair beside her, and he was afraid to speak lest he should scare away the hope her words gave him.

He merely said, "Well, well!" and waited for her to speak further. But her impulse had exhausted itself, as if her spirit were like one of those weak forms of life which spend their strength in a quick run or flight, and then rest to gather force for another. "Where's Boyne?" he asked, after waiting for her to speak.

"He was here a minute ago. He's been talking with some of the deck passengers that are going home because they couldn't get on in America. Doesn't that seem pitiful, poppa? I always thought we had work enough for the whole world."

"Perhaps these fellows didn't try very hard to find it," said the judge.

"Perhaps," she assented.

"I shouldn't want you to get to thinking that it's all like New York. Remember how comfortable everybody is in Tuskingum."

"Yes," she said, sadly. "How far off Tuskingum seems!"

"Well, don't forget about it; and remember that wherever life is simplest and purest and kindest, that is the highest civilization."

"How much like old times it seems to hear you talk that way, poppa! I should think I was in the library at home. And I made you leave it!" she sighed.

"Your mother was glad of any excuse. And it will do us all good, if we take it in the right way," said the judge, with a didactic severity that did not hide his pang from her.

"Poor poppa!" she said.

He went away, saying that he was going to look Lottie up. His simple design was to send Lottie to her mother, so that Breckon might come back to Ellen; but he did not own this to himself.

Lottie returned from another direction with Boyne, and Ellen said, "Poppa's gone to look for you."

"Has he?" asked Lottie, dropping decisively into her chair. "Well, there's one thing; I won't call him poppa any more."

"What will you call him?" Boyne demanded, demurely.

"I'll call him father, it you want to know; and I'm going to call momma, mother. I'm not going to have those English laughing at us, and I won't say papa and mamma. Everybody that knows anything says father and mother now."

Boyne kept looking from one sister to another during Lottie's declaration, and, with his eyes on Ellen, he said, "It's true, Ellen. All the Plumptons did." He was very serious.

Ellen smiled. "I'm too old to change. I'd rather seem queer in Europe than when I get back to Tuskingum."

"You wouldn't be queer there a great while," said Lottie. "They'll all be doing it in a week after I get home."

Upon the encouragement given him by Ellen, Boyne seized the chance of being of the opposition. "Yes," he taunted Lottie, "and you think they'll say woman and man, for lady and gentleman, I suppose."

"They will as soon as they know it's the thing."

"Well, I know I won't," said Boyne. "I won't call momma a woman."

"It doesn't matter what you do, Boyne dear," his sister serenely assured him.

While he stood searching his mind for a suitable retort, a young man, not apparently many years his senior, came round the corner of the music-room, and put himself conspicuously in view at a distance from the Kentons.

"There he is, now," said Boyne. "He wants to be introduced to Lottie." He referred the question to Ellen, but Lottie answered for her.

"Then why don't you introduce him?"

"Well, I would if he was an American. But you can't tell about these English." He resumed the dignity he had lost in making the explanation to Lottie, and ignored her in turning again to Ellen. "What do you think, Ellen?"

"Oh, don't know about such things, Boyne," she said, shrinking from the responsibility.

"Well; upon my word!" cried Lottie. "If Ellen can talk by the hour with that precious Mr. Breckon, and stay up here along with him, when everybody else is down below sick, I don't think she can have a great deal to say about a half-grown boy like that being introduced to me."

"He's as old as you are," said Boyne, hotly.

"Oh! I saw him associating with you, and I thought he was a boy, too. Pardon me!" Lottie turned from giving Boyne his coup-de-grace, to plant a little stab in Ellen's breast. "To be sure, now Mr. Breckon has found those friends of his, I suppose he won't want to flirt with Ellen any more."

"Ah, ha, ha!" Boyne broke in. "Lottie is mad because he stopped to speak to some ladies he knew. Women, I suppose she'd call them."

"Well, I shouldn't call him a gentleman, anyway," said Lottie.

The pretty, smooth-faced, fresh-faced young fellow whom their varying debate had kept in abeyance, looked round at them over his shoulder as he leaned on the rail, and seemed to discover Boyne for the first time. He came promptly towards the Kentons.

"Now," said Lottie, rapidly, "you'll just HAVE to."

The young fellow touched his cap to the whole group, but he ventured to address only Boyne.

"Every one seems to be about this morning," he said, with the cheery English-rising infection.

"Yes," answered Boyne, with such snubbing coldness that Ellen's heart was touched.

"It's so pleasant," she said, "after that dark weather."

"Isn't it?" cried the young fellow, gratefully. "One doesn't often get such sunshine as this at sea, you know."

"My sister, Miss Kenton, Mr. Pogis," Boyne solemnly intervened. "And Miss Lottie Kenton."

The pretty boy bowed to each in turn, but he made no pretence of being there to talk with Ellen. "Have you been ill, too?" he actively addressed himself to Lottie.

"No, just mad," she said. "I wasn't very sick, and that made it all the worse being down in a poky state-room when I wanted to walk."

"And I suppose you've been making up for lost time this morning?"

"Not half," said Lottie.

"Oh, do finish the half with me!"

Lottie instantly rose, and flung her sister the wrap she had been holding ready to shed from the moment the young man had come up. "Keep that for me, Nell. Are you good at catching?" she asked him.

"Catching?"

"Yes! People," she explained, and at a sudden twist of the ship she made a clutch at his shoulder.

"Oh! I think I can catch you."

As they moved off together, Boyne said, "Well, upon my word!" but Ellen did not say anything in comment on Lottie. After a while she asked, "Who were the ladies that Mr. Breckon met?"

"I didn't hear their names. They were somebody he hadn't seen before since the ship started. They looked like a young lady and her mother. It made Lottie mad when he stopped to speak with them, and she wouldn't wait till he could get through. Ran right away, and made me come, too."

XIII

Breckon had not seen the former interest between himself and Ellen lapse to commonplace acquaintance without due sense of loss. He suffered justly, but he did not suffer passively, or without several attempts to regain the higher ground. In spite of these he was aware of being distinctly kept to the level which he accused himself of having chosen, by a gentle acquiescence in his choice more fatal than snubbing. The advances that he made across the table, while he still met Miss Kenton alone there, did not carry beyond the rack supporting her plate. She talked on whatever subject he started with that angelic sincerity which now seemed so far from him, but she started none herself; she did not appeal to him for his opinion upon any question more psychological than the barometer; and,

"In a tumultuous privacy of storm,"

he found himself as much estranged from her as if a fair-weather crowd had surrounded them. He did not believe that she resented the levity he had shown; but he had reason to fear that she had finally accepted it as his normal mood, and in her efforts to meet him in it, as if he had no other, he read a tolerance that was worse than contempt. When he tried to make her think differently, if that was what she thought of him, he fancied her rising to the notion he wished to give her, and then shrinking from it, as if it must bring her the disappointment of some trivial joke.

It was what he had taught her to expect of him, and he had himself to blame. Now that he had thrown that precious chance away, he might well have overvalued it. She had certain provincialisms which he could not ignore. She did not know the right use of will and shall, and would and should, and she pronounced the letter 'r' with a hard mid-Western twist. Her voice was weak and thin, and she could not govern it from being at times a gasp and at times a drawl. She did not dress with the authority of women who know more of their clothes than the people they buy them of; she did not carry herself like a pretty girl; she had not the definite stamp of young-ladyism. Yet she was undoubtedly a lady in every instinct; she wore with pensive grace the clothes which she had not subjected to her personal taste; and if she did not carry herself like a pretty girl, she had a beauty which touched and entreated.

More and more Breckon found himself studying her beauty - her soft, brown brows, her gentle, dark eyes, a little sunken, and with the lids pinched by suffering; the cheeks somewhat thin, but not colorless; the long chin, the clear forehead, and the massed brown hair, that seemed too heavy for the drooping neck. It was not the modern athletic type; it was rather of the earlier period, when beauty was associated with the fragility despised by a tanned and golfing generation. Ellen Kenton's wrists were thin, and her hands long and narrow. As he looked at her across the racks during those two days of storm, he had sometimes the wish to take her long, narrow hands in his, and beg her to believe that he was worthier her serious friendship than he had shown himself. What he was sure of at all times now was that he wished to know the secret of that patient pathos of hers. She was not merely, or primarily, an invalid. Her family had treated her as an invalid, but, except Lottie, whose rigor might have been meant sanatively, they treated her more with the tenderness people use with a wounded spirit; and Breckon fancied moments of something like humility in her, when she seemed to cower from his notice. These were not so imaginable after her family took to their berths and left her alone with him, but the touching mystery remained, a sort of bewilderment, as he guessed it, a surprise such as a child might show at some incomprehensible harm. It was this grief which he had refused not merely to know - he still doubted his right to know it - but to share; he had denied not only his curiosity but his sympathy, and had exiled himself to a region where, when her family came back with the fair weather, he felt himself farther from her than before their acquaintance began.

He had made an overture to its renewal in the book he lent her, and then Mrs. Rasmith and her daughter had appeared on deck, and borne down upon him when he was walking with Lottie Kenton and trying to begin his self-retrieval through her. She had left him; but they had not, and in the bonds of a prophet and his followers he found himself bound with them for much more conversation than he had often held with them ashore. The parochial duties of an ethical teacher were not strenuous, and Breckon had not been made to feel them so definitely before. Mrs. Rasmith held that they now included promising to sit at her table for the rest of the voyage; but her daughter succeeded in releasing him from the obligation; and it was she who smilingly detached the clinging hold of the elder lady. "We mustn't keep Mr. Breckon from his friends, mother," she said, brightly, and then he said he should like the pleasure of introducing them, and both of the ladies declared that they would be delighted.

He bowed himself off, and half the ship's-length away he was aware, from meeting Lottie with her little Englishman, that it was she and not Ellen whom he was seeking. As the couple paused in whirring past Breckon long enough to let Lottie make her hat fast against the wind, he heard the Englishman shout:

"I say, that sister of yours is a fine girl, isn't she?"

"She's a pretty good - looker," Lottie answered back. "What's the matter with HER sister?"

"Oh, I say!" her companion returned, in a transport with her slangy pertness, which Breckon could not altogether refuse to share.

He thought that he ought to condemn it, and he did condemn Mrs. Kenton for allowing it in one of her daughters, when he came up to her sitting beside another whom he felt inexpressibly incapable of it. Mrs. Kenton could have answered his censure, if she had known it, that daughters, like sons, were not what their mothers but what their environments made them, and that the same environment sometimes made them different, as he saw. She could have told him that Lottie, with her slangy pertness, had the truest and best of the men she knew at her feet, and that Ellen, with her meekness, had been the prey of the commonest and cheapest spirit in her world, and so left him to make an inference as creditable to his sex as he could. But this bold defence was as far from the poor lady as any spoken reproach was from him. Her daughter had to check in her a mechanical offer to rise, as if to give Breckon her place, the theory and practice of Tuskingum being that their elders ought to leave young people alone together.

"Don't go, momma," Ellen whispered. "I don't want you to go."

Breckon, when he arrived before them, remained talking on foot, and, unlike Lottie's company, he talked to the mother. This had happened before from him, but she had not got used to it, and now she deprecated in everything but words his polite questions about her sufferings from the rough weather, and his rejoicing that the worst was probably over. She ventured the hope that it was so, for she said that Mr. Kenton had about decided to keep on to Holland, and it seemed to her that they had had enough of storms. He said he was glad that they were going right on; and then she modestly recurred to the earlier opinion he had given her husband that it would be better to spend the rest of the summer in Holland than to go to Italy, as if she wished to conform herself in the wisdom of Mr. Kenton's decision. He repeated his conviction, and he said that if he were in their place he should go to The Hague as soon as they had seen Rotterdam, and make it their headquarters for the exploration of the whole country.

"You can't realize how little it is; you can get anywhere in an hour; the difficulty is to keep inside of Holland when you leave any given point. I envy you going there."

Mrs. Kenton inferred that he was going to stop in France, but if it were part of his closeness not to tell, it was part of her pride not to ask. She relented when he asked if he might get a map of his and prove the littleness of Holland from it, and in his absence she could not well avoid saying to Ellen, "He seems very pleasant."

"Yes; why not?" the girl asked.

"I don't know. Lottie is so against him."

"He was very kind when you were all sick."

"Well, you ought to know better than Lottie; you've seen him so much more." Ellen was silent, and her mother advanced cautiously, "I suppose he is very cultivated."

"How can I tell? I'm not."

"Why, Ellen, I think you are. Very few girls have read so much."

"Yes, but he wouldn't care if I were cultivated, Ha is like all the rest. He would like to joke and laugh. Well, I think that is nice, too, and I wish I could do it. But I never could, and now I can't try. I suppose he wonders what makes me such a dead weight on you all."

"You know you're not that, Ellen! You musn't let yourself be morbid. It hurts me to have you say such things."

"Well, I should like to tell him why, and see what he

would say."

"Ellen!"

"Why not? If he is a minister he must have thought about all kinds of things. Do you suppose he ever knew of a girl before who had been through what I have? Yes, I would like to know what he would really say."

"I know what he ought to say! If he knew, he would say that no girl had ever behaved more angelically."

"Do you think he would? Perhaps he would say that if I hadn't been so proud and silly - Here he comes! Shall we ask him?"

Breckon approached with his map, and her mother gasped, thinking how terrible such a thing would be if it could be; Ellen smiled brightly up at him. "Will you take my chair? And then you can show momma your map. I am going down," and while he was still protesting she was gone.

"Miss Kenton seems so much better than she did the first day," he said, as he spread the map out on his knees, and gave Mrs. Kenton one end to hold.

"Yes," the mother assented, as she bent over to look at it.

She followed his explanation with a surface sense, while her nether mind was full of the worry of the question which Ellen had planted in it. What would such a man think of what she had been through? Or, rather, how would he say to her the only things that in Mrs. Kenton's belief he could say? How could the poor child ever be made to see it in the light of some mind not colored with her family's affection for her? An immense, an impossible longing possessed itself of the mother's heart, which became the more insistent the more frantic it appeared. She uttered "Yes" and "No" and "Indeed" to what he was saying, but all the time she was rehearsing Ellen's story in her inner sense. In the end she remembered so little what had actually passed that her dramatic reverie seemed the reality, and when she left him she got herself down to her state-room, giddy with the shame and fear of her imaginary self-betrayal. She wished to test the enormity, and yet not find it so monstrous, by submitting the case to her husband, and she could scarcely keep back her impatience at seeing Ellen instead of her father.

"Momma, what have you been saying to Mr. Breckon about me?"

"Nothing," said Mrs. Kenton, aghast at first, and then astonished to realize that she was speaking the simple truth. "He said how much better you were looking; but I don't believe I spoke a single word. We were looking at the map."

"Very well," Ellen resumed. "I have been thinking it all over, and now I have made up my mind."

She paused, and her mother asked, tremulously, "About what, Ellen?"

"You know, momma. I see all now. You needn't be afraid that I care anything about him now," and her mother knew that she meant Bittridge, "or that I ever shall. That's gone forever. But it's gone," she added, and her mother quaked inwardly to hear her reason, "because the wrong and the shame was all for me - for us. That's why I can forgive it, and forget. If we had done anything, the least thing in the world, to revenge ourselves, or to hurt him, then - Don't you see, momma?"

"I think I see, Ellen."

"Then I should have to keep thinking about it, and what we had made him suffer, and whether we hadn't given him some claim. I don't wish ever to think of him again. You and poppa were so patient and forbearing, all through; and I thank goodness now for everything you put up with; only I wish I could have borne everything myself."

"You had enough to bear," Mrs. Kenton said, in tender evasion.

"I'm glad that I had to bear so much, for bearing it is what makes me free now." She went up to her mother and kissed her, and gazed into her face with joyful, tearful looks that made her heart sink.

XIV

Mrs. Kenton did not rest till she had made sure from Lottie and Boyne that neither of them had dropped any hint to Ellen of what happened to Bittridge after his return to Tuskingum. She did not explain to them why she was so very anxious to know, but only charged them the more solemnly not to let the secret, which they had all been keeping from Ellen, escape them.

They promised, but Lottie said, "She's got to know it some time, and I should think the sooner the better."

"I will be judge of that, Lottie," said her mother, and Boyne seized his chance of inculpating her with his friend, Mr. Pogis. He said she was carrying on awfully with him already; and an Englishman could not understand, and Boyne hinted that he would presume upon her American freedom.

"Well, if he does, I'll get you to cowhide him, Boyne," she retorted, and left him fuming helplessly, while she went to give the young Englishman an opportunity of resuming the flirtation which her mother had interrupted.

With her husband Mrs. Kenton found it practicable to be more explicit. "I haven't had such a load lifted off my heart since I don't know when. It shows me what I've thought all along: that Ellen hasn't really cared anything for that miserable thing since he first began going with Mrs. Uphill a year ago. When he wrote that letter to her in New York she wanted to

William Dean Howells

be sure she didn't, and when he offered himself and misbehaved so to both of you, she was afraid that she and you were somehow to blame. Now she's worked it out that no one else was wronged, and she is satisfied. It's made her feel free, as she says. But, oh, dear me!" Mrs. Kenton broke off, "I talk as if there was nothing to bind her; and yet there is what poor Richard did! What would she say if she knew that? I have been cautioning Lottie and Boyne, but I know it will come out somehow. Do you think it's wise to keep it from her? Hadn't we better tell her? Or shall we wait and see -"

Kenton would not allow to her or to himself that his hopes ran with hers; love is not business with a man as it is with a woman; he feels it indecorous and indelicate to count upon it openly, where she thinks it simply a chance of life, to be considered like another. All that Kenton would say was, "I see no reason for telling her just yet. She will have to know in due time. But let her enjoy her freedom now."

"Yes," Mrs. Kenton doubtfully assented.

The judge was thoughtfully silent. Then he said: "Few girls could have worked out her problem as Ellen has. Think how differently Lottie would have done it!"

"Lottie has her good points, too," said Mrs. Kenton. "And, of course, I don't blame Richard. There are all kinds of girls, and Lottie means no more harm than Ellen does. She's the kind that can't help attracting; but I always knew that Ellen was attractive, too, if she would only find it out. And I knew that as soon as anything worth while took up her mind she would never give that wretch another thought."

Kenton followed her devious ratiocinations to a conclusion which he could not grasp. "What do you mean, Sarah?"

"If I only," she explained, in terms that did not explain, "felt as sure of him as I do about him!"

Her husband looked densely at her. "Bittridge?"

"No. Mr. Breckon. He is very nice, Rufus. Yes, he is! He's been showing me the map of Holland, and we've had a long talk. He isn't the way we thought - or I did. He is not at all clerical, or worldly. And he appreciates Ellen. I don't suppose he cares so much for her being cultivated; I suppose she doesn't seem so to him. But he sees how wise she is - how good. And he couldn't do that without being good himself! Rufus! If we could only hope such a thing. But, of course, there are thousands after him!"

"There are not thousands of Ellens after him," said the judge, before he could take time to protest. "And I don't want him to suppose that she is after him at all. If he will only interest her and help her to keep her mind off herself, it's all I will ask of him. I am not anxious to part with her, now that she's all ours again."

"Of course," Mrs. Kenton soothingly assented. "And I don't say that she dreams of him in any such way. She can't help admiring his mind. But what I mean is that when you see how he appreciates her, you can't help wishing he could know just how wise, and just how good she is. It did seem to me as if I would give almost anything to have him know what she had been through with that - rapscallion!"

"Sarah!"

"Oh, you may Sarah me! But I can tell you what, Mr. Kenton: I believe that you could tell him every word of it, and only make him appreciate her the more. Till you know that about Ellen, you don't know what a character she is. I just ached to tell him!"

"I don't understand you, my dear," said Kenton. "But if you mean to tell him -"

"Why, who could imagine doing such a thing? Don't you see

that it is impossible? Such a thing would never have come into my head if it hadn't been for some morbid talk of Ellen's."

"Of Ellen's?"

"Oh, about wanting to disgust him by telling him why she was such a burden to us."

"She isn't a burden!"

"I am saying what she said. And it made me think that if such a person could only know the high-minded way she had found to get out of her trouble! I would like somebody who is capable of valuing her to value her in all her preciousness. Wouldn't you be glad if such a man as he is could know how and why she feels free at last?"

"I don't think it's necessary," said Kenton, haughtily, "There's only one thing that could give him the right to know it, and we'll wait for that first. I thought you said that he was frivolous."

"Boyne said that, and Lottie. I took it for granted, till I talked with him to-day. He is light-hearted and gay; he likes to laugh and joke; but he can be very serious when he wants to."

"According to all precedent," said the judge, glumly, "such a man ought to be hanging round Lottie. Everybody was that amounted to anything in Tuskingum."

"Oh, in Tuskingum! And who were the men there that amounted to anything? A lot of young lawyers, and two students of medicine, and some railroad clerks. There wasn't one that would compare with Mr. Breckon for a moment."

"All the more reason why he can't really care for Ellen. Now see here, Sarah! You know I don't interfere with you and the children, but I'm afraid you're in a craze about this young fellow. He's got these friends of his who have just turned up, and we'll wait and see what he does with them. I guess he appreciates the young lady as much as he does Ellen."

Mrs. Kenton's heart went down. "She doesn't compare with Ellen!" she piteously declared.

"That's what we think. He may think differently."

Mrs. Kenton was silenced, but all the more she was determined to make sure that Mr. Breckon was not interested in Miss Rasmith in any measure or manner detrimental to Ellen. As for Miss Rasmith herself, Mrs. Kenton would have had greater reason to be anxious about her behavior with Boyne than Mr. Breckon. From the moment that the minister had made his two groups of friends acquainted, the young lady had fixed upon Boyne as that member of the Kenton group who could best repay a more intimate friendship. She was polite to them all, but to Boyne she was flattering, and he was too little used to deference from ladies ten years his senior not to be very sensible of her worth in offering it. To be unremittingly treated as a grown-up person was an experience so dazzling that his vision was blinded to any possibilities in the behavior that formed it; and before the day ended Boyne had possessed Miss Rasmith of all that it was important for any fellow-being to know of his character and history. He opened his heart to eyes that had looked into others before his, less for the sake of exploiting than of informing himself. In the rare intelligence of Miss Rasmith he had found that serious patience with his problems which no one else, not Ellen herself, had shown, and after trying her sincerity the greater part of the day he put it to the supreme test, one evening, with a book which he had been reading. Boyne's literature was largely entomological and zoological, but this was a work of fiction treating of the fortunes of a young American adventurer, who had turned his military education to account in the service of a German princess. Her Highness's dominions were not in any map of Europe, and perhaps it was her condition of political incognito that rendered her the more fittingly the prey of a passion for the American head of her armies. Boyne's belief was that this character veiled a real identity, and he wished to submit to Miss Rasmith the question whether in the exclusive circles of New York society any young millionaire was known to have taken service abroad after leaving west Point. He put it in the form of a scoffing incredulity which it was a comfort to have her take as if almost hurt by his doubt. She said that such a thing might very well be, and with rich American girls marrying all sorts of titles abroad, it was not impossible for some brilliant young fellow to make his way to the steps of a throne. Boyne declared that she was laughing at him, and she protested that it was the last thing she should think of doing; she was too much afraid of him. Then he began to argue against the case supposed in the romance; he proved from the book itself that the thing could not happen; such a princess would not be allowed to marry the American, no matter how rich he was. She owned that she had not heard of just such an instance, and he might think her very romantic; and perhaps she was; but if the princess was an absolute princess, such as she was shown in that story, she held that no power on earth could keep her from marrying the young American. For herself she did not see, though, how the princess could be in love with that type of American. If she had been in the princess's place she should have fancied something quite different. She made Boyne agree with her that Eastern Americans were all, more or less, Europeanized, and it stood to reason, she held, that a European princess would want something as un-European as possible if she was falling in love to please herself. They had some contention upon the point that the princess would want a Western American; and then Miss Rasmith, with a delicate audacity, painted an heroic portrait of Boyne himself which he could not recognize openly enough to disown; but he perceived resemblances in it which went to his head when she demurely rose, with a soft "Good-night, Mr. Kenton. I suppose I mustn't call you Boyne?"

"Oh yes, do!" he entreated. "I'm-I'm not grown up yet, you know."

"Then it will be safe," she sighed. "But I should never have thought of that. I had got so absorbed in our argument. You are so logical, Mr. Kenton - Boyne, I mean - thank you. You must get it from your father. How lovely your sister is!"

"Ellen?"

"Well, no. I meant the other one. But Miss Kenton is beautiful, too. You must be so happy together, all of you." She added, with a rueful smile, "There's only one of me! Good-night."

Boyne did not know whether he ought not in humanity, if not gallantry, to say he would be a brother to her, but while he stood considering, she put out a hand to him so covered with rings that he was afraid she had hurt herself in pressing his so hard, and had left him before he could decide.

Lottie, walking the deck, had not thought of bidding Mr. Pogis good-night. She had asked him half a dozen times how late it was, and when he answered, had said as often that she knew better, and she was going below in another minute. But she stayed, and the flow of her conversation supplied him with occasion for the remarks of which he seldom varied the formula. When she said something too audacious for silent emotion, he called out, "Oh, I say!" If she advanced an opinion too obviously acceptable, or asked a question upon some point where it seemed to him there could not be two minds, he was ready with the ironical note, "Well, rather!" At times she pressed her studies of his character and her observations on his manner and appearance so far that he was forced to protest, "You are so personal!" But these moments were rare; for the most part, "Oh I say!" and "Well, rather!" perfectly covered the ground. He did not generally mind her parody of his poverty of phrase, but once, after she had repeated "Well rather!" and "Oh, I say!" steadily at everything he said for the whole round of the promenade they were making, he intimated that there were occasions when, in his belief, a woman's abuse of the freedom generously allowed her sex passed the point of words.

"And when it passes the point of words" she taunted him, "what do you do?"

"You will see," he said, "if it ever does," and Lottie felt justified by her inference that he was threatening to kiss her, in answering:

"And if I ever SEE, I will box your ears."

"Oh, I say!" he retorted. "I should like to have you try."

He had ideas of the rightful mastery of a man in all things, which she promptly pronounced brutal, and when he declared that his father's conduct towards his wife and children was based upon these ideas, she affirmed the superiority of her own father's principles and behavior. Mr. Pogis was too declared an admirer of Judge Kenton to question his motives or method in anything, and he could only generalize, "The Americans spoil their women."

"Well, their women are worth it," said Lottie, and after allowing the paradox time to penetrate his intelligence, he cried out, in a glad transport:

"Oh, I SAY!"

At the moment Boyne's intellectual seance with Miss Rasmith was coming to an end. Lottie had tacitly invited Mr. Pogis to prolong the comparison of English and American family life by stopping in front of a couple of steamer-chairs, and confessing that she was tired to death. They sat down, and he told her about his mother, whom, although his father's subordinate, he seemed to be rather fonder of. He had some elder brothers, most of them in the colonies, and he had himself been out to America looking at something his father had found for him in Buffalo.

"You ought to come to Tuskingum," said Lottie.

"Is that a large place?" Mr. Pogis asked. "As large as Buffalo?"

"Well, no," Lottie admitted. "But it's a growing place. And we have the best kind of times."

"What kind?" The young man easily consented to turn the commercial into a social inquiry.

"Oh, picnics, and river parties, and buggy-rides, and dances."

"I'm keen on dancing," said Mr. Pogis. "I hope they'll give us a dance on board. Will you put me down for the first dance?"

"I don't care. Will you send me some flowers? The steward must have some left in the refrigerator."

"Well, rather! I'll send you a spray, if he's got enough."

"A spray? What's a spray?"

"Oh, I say! My sister always wears one. It's a long chain of flowers reachin' from your shoulder diagonally down to your waist."

"Does your sister always have her sprays sent to her?"

"Well, rather! Don't they send flowers to girls for dances in the States?"

"Well, rather! Didn't I just ask you?"

This was very true, and after a moment of baffle Mr. Pogis said, in generalization, "If you go with a young lady in a party to the theatre you send her a box of chocolates."

"Only when you go to theatre! I couldn't get enough, then, unless you asked me every night," said Lottie, and while Mr. Pogis was trying to choose between "Oh, I say!" and something specific, like, "I should like to ask you every night," she added,

"And what would happen if you sent a girl a spray for the theatre and chocolates for a dance? Wouldn't it jar her?"

Now, indeed, there was nothing for him but to answer, "Oh, I say!"

"Well, say, then! Here comes Boyne, and I must go. Well, Boyne," she called, from the dark nook where she sat, to her brother as he stumbled near, with his eyes to the stars, "has the old lady retired?"

He gave himself away finely. "What old lady!"

"Well, maybe at your age you don't consider her very old. But I don't think a boy ought to sit up mooning at his grandmother all night. I know Miss Rasmith's no relation, if that's what you're going to say!"

"Oh, I say!" Mr. Pogis chuckled. "You are so personal."

"Well, rather!" said Lottie, punishing his presumption. "But I don't think it's nice for a kid, even if she isn't."

"Kid!" Boyne ground, through his clenched teeth.

By this time Lottie was up out of her chair and beyond repartee in her flight down the gangway stairs. She left the two youngsters confronted.

"What do you say to a lemon-squash?" asked Mr. Pogis, respecting his friend's wounded dignity, and ignoring Lottie and her offence.

"I don't care if I do," said Boyne in gloomy acquiescence.

XV

Few witnesses of the fact that Julia Rasmith and her mother had found themselves on the same steamer with the Rev. Hugh Breckon would have been of such a simple mind as to think they were there by accident, if they had also been witnesses of their earlier history. The ladies could have urged that in returning from California only a few days before the Amstel sailed, and getting a state-room which had been unexpectedly given up, they had some claim to a charitable interpretation of their behavior, but this plea could not have availed them with any connoisseur of women. Besides, it had been a matter of notoriety among such of Mr. Breckon's variegated congregation as knew one another that Mrs. Rasmith had set her heart on him, it Julia had not set her cap for him. In that pied flock, where every shade and dapple of doubt, from heterodox Jew to agnostic Christian, foregathered, as it has been said, in the misgiving of a blessed immortality, the devotion of Mrs. Rasmith to the minister had been almost a scandal. Nothing had saved the appearance from this character but Mr. Breckon's open acceptance of her flatteries and hospitalities; this was so frank, and the behavior of Julia herself so judicious under the circumstances, that envy and virtue were, if not equally silenced, equally baffled. So far from pretending not to see her mother's manoeuvres, Julia invited public recognition of them; in the way of joking, which she kept within the limits of filial fondness, she made fun of her mother's infatuation to Breckon himself, and warned him against the moment when her wiles might be too much for him. Before other people she did not hesitate to save him from her mother, so that even

William Dean Howells

those who believed her in the conspiracy owned that no girl could have managed with more cleverness in a situation where not every one would have refused to be placed. In this situation Julia Rasmith had the service of a very clear head, and as was believed by some, a cool heart; if she and her mother had joint designs upon the minister, hers was the ambition, and her mother's the affection that prompted them. She was a long, undulant girl, of a mixed blondness that left you in doubt, after you had left her, whether her hair or her complexion were not of one tint; but her features were good, and there could be no question of her captivating laugh, and her charming mouth, which she was always pulling down with demure irony. She was like her mother in her looks, but her indolent, droning temperament must have been from her father, whose memory was lost in that antiquity which swallows up the record of so many widows' husbands, and who could not have left her what was left of her mother's money, for none of it had ever been his. It was still her mother's, and it was supposed to be the daughter's chief attraction. There must, therefore, have been a good deal of it, for those who were harshest with the minister did not believe that a little money would attract him. Not that they really thought him mercenary; some of his people considered him gay to the verge of triviality, but there were none that accused him of insincerity. They would have liked a little more seriousness in him, especially when they had not much of their own, and would have had him make up in severity of behavior for what he lacked, and what they wished him to lack, in austerity of doctrine.

The Amstel had lost so much time in the rough weather of her first days out that she could not make it up with her old-fashioned single screw. She was at best a ten-day boat, counting from Sandy Hook to Boulogne, and she had not been four days out when she promised to break her record for slowness. Three days later Miss Rasmith said to Breckon, as he took the chair which her mother agilely abandoned to him beside her: "The head steward says it will be a twelve-day trip, end our bedroom steward thinks more. What is the consensus of opinion in the smoking-room? Where are you going, mother? Are you planning to leave Mr. Breckon and me alone again? It isn't necessary. We couldn't get away from each other if we tried, and all we ask - Well, I suppose age must be indulged in its little fancies," she called after Mrs. Rasmith.

Breckon took up the question she had asked him. "The odds are so heavily in favor of a fifteen-days' run that there are no takers."

"Now you are joking again," she said. "I thought a sea-voyage might make you serious."

"It has been tried before. Besides, it's you that I want to be serious."

"What about? Besides, I doubt it."

"About Boyne."

"Oh! I thought you were going to say some one else."

"No, I think that is very well settled."

"You'll never persuade my mother," said Miss Rasmith, with a low, comfortable laugh.

"But if you are satisfied -"

"She will have to resign herself? Well, perhaps. But why do you wish me to be serious about Boyne?"

"I have no doubt he amuses you. But that doesn't seem a very good reason why you should amuse yourself with him."

"No? Why not?"

"Well, because the poor boy is in earnest; and you're not exactly - contemporaries."

"Why, how old is Boyne?" she asked, with affected surprise.

"About fifteen, I think," said Breckon, gravely.

"And I'm but a very few months past thirty. I don't see the great disparity. But he is merely a brother to me - an elder brother - and he gives me the best kind of advice."

"I dare say you need it, but all the same, I am afraid you are putting ideas into his head."

"Well, if he began it? If he put them in mine first?"

She was evidently willing that he should go further, and create the common ground between them that grows up when one gives a reproof and the other accepts it; but Breckon, whether he thought that he had now done his duty, and need say no more, or because he was vexed with her, left the subject.

"Mrs. Rasmith says you are going to Switzerland for the rest of the summer."

"Yes, to Montreux. Are you going to spend it in Paris?"

"I'm going to Paris to see. I have had some thoughts of Etretat; I have cousins there."

"I wish that I could go to the sea-side. But this happens to be one of the summers when nothing but mountains can save my mother's life. Shall you get down to Rome before you go back?"

"I don't know. If I sail from Naples I shall probably pass through Rome."

"You had better stop off. We shall be there in November, and they say Rome is worth seeing," she laughed demurely. "That is what Boyne understands. He's promised to use his influence with his family to let him run down to see us there, if he can't get them all to come. You might offer to personally conduct them."

"Yes." said Breckon, with the effect of cloture. "Have you made many acquaintances an board?"

"What! Two lone women? You haven't introduced us to any but the Kentons. But I dare say they are the best. The judge is a dear, and Mrs. Kenton is everything that is motherly and matronly. Boyne says she is very well informed, and knows all about the reigning families. If he decides to marry into them, she can be of great use in saving him from a mesalliance. I can't say very much for Miss Lottie. Miss Lottie seems to me distinctly of the minx type. But that poor, pale girl is adorable. I wish she liked me!"

"What makes you think she doesn't like you?" Breckon asked.

"What? Women don't require anything to convince them that other women can't bear them. They simply know it. I wonder what has happened to her?"

"Why do you think anything has happened to her?"

"Why? Well, girls don't have that air of melanholy absence for nothing. She is brooding upon something, you may be sure. But you have had so many more opportunities than I! Do you mean that you haven't suspected a tragical past far her?"

"I don't know," said Breckon, a little restively, "that I have allowed myself to speculate about her past."

"That is, you oughtn't to have allowed yourself to do so. Well, there I agree with you. But a woman may do so without impertinence, and I am sure that Miss Kenton has a story. I have watched her, and her face has told me everything but the story."

Breckon would not say that some such revelation had been

William Dean Howells

made to him, and in the absence of an answer from him Miss Rasmith asked, "Is she cultivated, too?"

"Too?"

"Like her mother."

"Oh! I should say she had read a good dial. And she's bookish, yes, in a simple-hearted kind of way."

"She asks you if you have read 'the book of the year,' and whether you don't think the heroine is a beautiful character?"

"Not quite so bad as that. But if you care to be serious about her!"

"Oh, I do!"

"I doubt it. Then, I should say that she seems to have grown up in a place where the interests are so material that a girl who was disposed to be thoughtful would be thrown back upon reading for her society more than in more intellectual centres - if there are such things. She has been so much with books that she does not feel odd in speaking of them as if they were the usual topics of conversation. It gives her a certain quaintness."

"And that is what constitutes her charm?"

"I didn't know that we were speaking of her charm."

"No, that is true. But I was thinking of it. She fascinates me. Are they going to get off at Boulogne?"

"No, they are going on to Rotterdam."

"To be sure! Boyne told me. And are you going on with them?"

"I thought we talked of my going to Paris." Breckon looked

round at her, and she made a gesture of deprecation.

"Why, of course! How could I forget? But I'm so much interested in Miss Kenton that I can't think of anything else."

"Not even of Miss Rasmith?"

"Not even of Miss Rasmith. I know that she has a history, and that it's a sad one." She paused in ironical hesitation. "You've been so good as to caution me about her brother - and I never can be grateful enough - and that makes me almost free to suggest -"

She stopped again, and he asked, hardily, "What?"

"Oh, nothing. It isn't for me to remind my pastor, my ghostly adviser" - she pulled down her mouth and glanced at him demurely - "and I will only offer the generalization that a girl is never so much in danger of having her heart broken as when she's had it broken - Oh, are you leaving me?" she cried, as Breckon rose from his chair.

"Well, then, send Boyne to me." She broke into a laugh as he faltered. "Are you going to sit down again? That is right. And I won't talk any more about Miss Kenton."

"I don't mind talking of her," said Breckon. "Perhaps it will even be well to do so if you are in earnest. Though it strikes me that you have rather renounced the right to criticise me."

"Now, is that logical? It seems to me that in putting myself in the attitude of a final friend at the start, and refusing to be anything more, I leave established my right to criticise you on the firmest basis. I can't possibly be suspected of interested motives. Besides, you've just been criticizing me, if you want a woman's reason!"

"Well, go on."

"Why, I had finished. That's the amusing part. I should have supposed that I could go on forever about Miss Kenton, but I have nothing to go upon. She has kept her secret very well, and so have the rest of them. You think I might have got it out of Boyne? Perhaps I might, but you know I have my little scruples. I don't think it would be quite fair, or quite nice."

"You are scrupulous. And I give you credit for having been more delicate than I've been."

"You don't mean you've been trying to find it out!"

"Ah, now I'm not sure about the superior delicacy!"

"Oh, how good!" said Miss Rasmith. "What a pity you should be wasted in a calling that limits you so much."

"You call it limiting? I didn't know but I had gone too far."

"Not at all! You know there's nothing I like so much as those little digs."

"I had forgotten. Then you won't mind my saying that this surveillance seems to me rather more than I have any right to from you."

"How exquisitely you put it! Who else could have told me to mind my own business so delightfully? Well, it isn't my business. I acknowledge that, and I spoke only because I knew you would be sorry if you had gone too far. I remembered our promise to be friends."

She threw a touch of real feeling into her tone, and he responded, "Yes, and I thank you for it, though it isn't easy."

She put out her hand to him, and, as he questioningly took it, she pressed his with animation. "Of course it isn't! Or it wouldn't be for any other man. But don't you suppose I appreciate that supreme courage of yours? There is nobody else-nobody! - who could stand up to an impertinence and turn it to praise by such humility."

"Don't go too far, or I shall be turning your praise to impertinence by my humility. You're quite right, though, about the main matter. I needn't suppose anything so preposterous as you suggest, to feel that people are best left alone to outlive their troubles, unless they are of the most obvious kind."

"Now, if I thought I had done anything to stop you from offering that sort of helpfulness which makes you a blessing to everybody, I should never forgive myself."

"Nothing so dire as that, I believe. But if you've made me question the propriety of applying the blessing in all cases, you have done a very good thing."

Miss Rasmith was silent and apparently serious. After a moment she said, "And I, for my part, promise to let poor little Boyne alone."

Breckon laughed. "Don't burlesque it! Besides, I haven't promised anything."

"That is very true," said Miss Rasmith, and she laughed, too.

XVI

In one of those dramatic reveries which we all hold with ourselves when fortune has pressingly placed us, Ellen Kenton had imagined it possible for her to tell her story to the man who had so gently and truly tried to be her friend. It was mostly in the way of explaining to him how she was unworthy of his friendship that the story was told, and she fancied telling it without being scandalized at violating the conventions that should have kept her from even dreaming of such a thing. It was all exalted to a plane where there was no question of fit or unfit in doing it, but only the occasion; and he would never hear of the unworthiness which she wished to ascribe to herself. Sometimes he mournfully left her when she persisted, left her forever, and sometimes he refused, and retained with her in a sublime kindness, a noble amity, lofty and serene, which did not seek to become anything else. In this case she would break from her reveries with self-accusing cries, under her breath, of "Silly, silly! Oh, how disgusting!" and if at that moment Breckon were really coming up to sit by her, she would blush to her hair, and wish to run away, and failing the force for this, would sit cold and blank to his civilities, and have to be skilfully and gradually talked back to self-respect and self-tolerance.

The recurrence of these reveries and their consequence in her made it difficult for him to put in effect the promise he had given himself in Miss Rasmith's presence. If Ellen had been eager to welcome his coming, it would have been very simple to keep away from her, but as she appeared anxious to escape him, and had to be entreated, as it were, to suffer his society, something better than his curiosity was piqued, though that was piqued, too. He believed that he saw her lapsing again into that morbid state from which he had seemed once able to save her, and he could not help trying again. He was the more bound to do so by the ironical observance of Miss Rasmith, who had to be defied first, and then propitiated; certainly, when she saw him apparently breaking faith with her, she had a right to some sort of explanation, but certainly also she had no right to a blind and unreasoning submission from him. His embarrassment was heightened by her interest in Miss Kenton, whom, with an admirable show of now finding her safe from Breckon's attractions, she was always wishing to study from his observation. What was she really like? The girl had a perfect fascination for her; she envied him his opportunities of knowing her, and his privileges of making that melancholy face light up with that heart-breaking smile, and of banishing that delicious shyness with which she always seemed to meet him. Miss Rasmith had noticed it; how could she help noticing it?

Breckon wished to himself that she had been able to help noticing it, or were more capable of minding her own business than she showed herself, and his heart closed about Ellen with a tenderness that was dangerously indignant. At the same time he felt himself withheld by Miss Rasmith's witness from being all to the girl that he wished to be, and that he now seemed to have been in those first days of storm, while Miss Rasmith and her mother were still keeping their cabin. He foresaw that it would end in Miss Rasmith's sympathetic nature not being able to withhold itself from Ellen's need of cheerful companionship, and he was surprised, as little as he was pleased, one morning, when he came to take the chair beside her to find Miss Rasmith in it, talking and laughing to the girl, who perversely showed herself amused. Miss Rasmith made as if to offer him the seat, but he had to go away disappointed, after standing long enough before them to be aware that they were suspending some topic while he stayed.

He naturally supposed the topic to be himself, but it was not so, or at least not directly so. It was only himself as related to the scolding he had given Miss Rasmith for trifling with the innocence of Boyne, which she wished Miss Kenton to understand as the effect of a real affection for her brother. She loved all boys, and Boyne was simply the most delightful creature in the world. She went on to explain how delightful he was, and showed a such an appreciation of the infantile sweetness mingled with the mature severity of Boyne's character that Ellen could not help being pleased and won. She told some little stories of Boyne that threw a light also their home life in Tuskingum, and Miss Rasmith declared herself perfectly fascinated, and wished that she could go and live in Tuskingum. She protested that she should not find it dull; Boyne alone would be entertainment enough; and she figured a circumstance so idyllic from the hints she had gathered, that Ellen's brow darkened in silent denial, and Miss Rasmith felt herself, as the children say in the game, very hot in her proximity to the girl's secret. She would have liked to know it, but whether she felt that she could know it when she liked enough, or whether she should not be so safe with Breckon in knowing it, she veered suddenly away, and said that she was so glad to have Boyne's family know the peculiar nature of her devotion, which did not necessarily mean running away with him, though it might come to that. She supposed she was a little morbid about it from what Mr. Breckon had been saying; he had a conscience that would break the peace of a whole community, though he was the greatest possible favorite, not only with his own congregation, which simply worshipped him, but with the best society, where he was in constant request.

It was not her fault if she did not overdo these history, but perhaps it was all true about the number of girls who were ready and willing to marry him. It might even be true, though she had no direct authority for saying it, that he had made up his mind never to marry, and that was the reason why he felt himself so safe in being the nicest sort of friend. He was safe, Miss Rasmith philosophized, but whether other people were so safe was a different question. There were girls who were said to be dying for him; but of course those things were always said about a handsome young minister. She had frankly taken him on his own ground, from the beginning, and she believed that this was what he liked. At any rate, they had agreed that they were never to be anything but the best of friends, and they always had been.

Mrs. Kenton came and shyly took the chair on Miss Rasmith's other side, and Miss Rasmith said they had been talking about Mr. Breckon, and she repeated what she had been saying to Ellen. Mrs. Kenton assented more openly than Ellen could to her praises, but when she went away, and her daughter sat passive, without comment or apparent interest, the mother drew a long, involuntary sigh.

"Do you like her, Ellen?"

"She tries to be pleasant, I think."

"Do you think she really knows much about Mr. Breckon?"

"Oh yes. Why not? She belongs to his church."

"He doesn't seem to me like a person who would have a parcel of girls tagging after him."

"That is what they do in the East, Boyne says."

"I wish she would let Boyne alone. She is making a fool of the child. He's round with her every moment. I think she ought to be ashamed, such an old thing!"

Ellen chose to protest, or thought it fair to do so. "I don't believe she is doing him any harm. She just lets him talk out, and everybody else checks him up so. It was nice of her to come and talk with me, when we had all been keeping away from her. Perhaps he sent her, though. She says they have always been such good friends because she wouldn't be anything else from the beginning."

"I don't see why she need have told you that."

"Oh, it was just to show he was run after. I wonder if he thinks we are running after him? Momma, I am tired of him! I wish he wouldn't speak to me any more."

"Why! do you really dislike him, Ellen?"

"No, not dislike him. But it tires me to have him trying to amuse me. Don't you understand?"

Mrs. Kenton said yes, she understood, but she was clear only of the fact that Ellen seemed flushed and weak at that moment. She believed that it was Miss Rasmith and not Mr. Breckon who was to blame, but she said: "Well, you needn't worry about it long. It will only be a day or two now till we get to Boulogne, and then he will leave us. Hadn't you better go down now, and rest awhile in your berth? I will bring your things."

Ellen rose, pulling her wraps from her skirts to give them to her mother. A voice from behind said between their meeting shoulders: "Oh, are you going down? I was just coming to beg Miss Kenton to take a little walk with me," and they looked round together and met Breckon's smiling face.

"I'm afraid," Mrs. Kenton began, and then, like a well-trained American mother, she stopped and left the affair to her daughter.

"Do you think you can get down with them, momma?" the girl asked, and somehow her mother's heart was lightened by her evasion, not to call it uncandor. It was at least not morbid, it was at least like other girls, and Mrs. Kenton imparted what comfort there was in it to the judge, when he asked where she had left Ellen.

"Not that it's any use," she sighed, when she had seen him share it with a certain shamefacedness. "That woman has got her grip on him, and she doesn't mean to let go."

Kenton understood Miss Rasmith by that woman; but he would not allow himself to be so easily cast down. This was one of the things that provoked Mrs. Kenton with him; when he had once taken hope he would not abandon it without reason. "I don't see any evidence of her having her grip on him. I've noticed him, and he doesn't seem attentive to her. I should say he tried to avoid her. He certainly doesn't avoid Ellen."

"What are you thinking of, Rufus?"

"What are you? You know we'd both be glad if he fancied her."

"Well, suppose we would? I don't deny it. He is one of the most agreeable gentlemen I ever saw; one of the kindest and nicest."

"He's more than that," said the judge. "I've been sounding him on various points, and I don't see where he's wrong. Of course, I don't know much about his religious persuasion, if it is one, but I think I'm a pretty fair judge of character, and that young man has character. He isn't a light person, though he likes joking and laughing, and he appreciates Ellen."

"Yes, so do we. And there's about as much prospect of his marrying her. Rufus, it's pretty hard! She's just in the mood to be taken with him, but she won't let herself, because she knows it's of no use. That Miss Rasmith has been telling her how much he is run after, and I could see that that settled it for Ellen as plainly as if she said so. More plainly, for there's enough of the girl in her to make her say one thing when she means another. She was just saying she was sick of him, and never wanted to speak to him again, when he came up and asked her to walk, and she went with him instantly. I knew what she meant. She wasn't going to let him suppose that anything Miss Rasmith had said was going to change her."

"Well, then," said the judge, "I don't see what you're scared at."

"I'm not SCARED. But, oh, Rufus! It can't come to anything! There isn't time!" An hysterical hope trembled in her asseveration of despair that made him smile.

"I guess if time's all that's wanted -"

"He is going to get off at Boulogne."

"Well, we can get off there, too."

"Rufus, if you dare to think of such a thing!"

"I don't. But Europe isn't so big but what he can find us again if he wants to."

"Ah, if he wants to!"

Ellen seemed to have let her mother take her languor below along with the shawls she had given her. Buttoned into a close jacket, and skirted short for the sea, she pushed against the breeze at Breckon's elbow with a vigor that made him look his surprise at her. Girl-like, she took it that something was wrong with her dress, and ran herself over with an uneasy eye.

Then he explained: "I was just thinking how much you were like Miss Lottie-if you'll excuse my being so personal. And it never struck me before."

"I didn't suppose we looked alike," said Ellen.

"No, certainly. I shouldn't have taken you for sisters. And yet, just now, I felt that you were like her. You seem so much stronger this morning - perhaps it's that the voyage is doing you good. Shall you be sorry to have it end?"

"Shall you? That's the way Lottie would answer."

Breckon laughed. "Yes, it is. I shall be very sorry. I should be willing to have it rough again, it that would make it longer. I liked it's being rough. We had it to ourselves." He had not thought how that sounded, but if it sounded particular, she did not notice it.

She merely said, "I was surprised not to be seasick, too."

"And should you be willing to have it rough again?"

"You wouldn't see anything more of your friends, then."

"Ah, yes; Miss Rasmith. She is a great talker, Did you find her interesting?"

"She was very interesting."

"Yes? What did she talk about?"

Ellen realized the fact too late to withhold "Why, about you."

"And was that what made her interesting?"

"Now, what would Lottie say to such a thing as that?" asked Ellen, gayly.

"Something terribly cutting, I'm afraid. But don't you! From you I don't want to believe I deserve it, no matter what Miss Rasmith said me."

"Oh, she didn't say anything very bad. Unless you mind being a universal favorite."

"Well, it makes a man out rather silly."

"But you can't help that."

"Now you remind me of Miss Lottie again!"

"But I didn't mean that," said Ellen, blushing and laughing. "I hope you wouldn't think I could be so pert."

"I wouldn't think anything that wasn't to your praise," said Breckon, and a pause ensued, after which the words he added seemed tame and flat. "I suspect Miss Rasmith has been idealizing the situation. At any rate, I shouldn't advise you to trust her report implicitly. I'm at the head of a society, you know, ethical or sociological, or altruistic, whatever you choose to call it, which hasn't any very definite object of worship, and yet meets every Sunday for a sort of worship; and I have to be in the pulpit. So you see?"

Ellen said, "I think I understand," with a temptation to smile at the ruefulness of his appeal.

Breckon laughed for her. "That's the mischief and the absurdity of it. But it isn't so bad as it seems. They're really most of them hard-headed people; and those that are not couldn't make a fool of a man that nature hadn't begun with. Still, I'm not very well satisfied with my work among them - that is, I'm not satisfied with myself." He was talking soberly enough, and he did not find that she was listening too seriously. "I'm going away to see whether I shall come back." He looked at her to make sure that she had taken his meaning, and seemed satisfied that she had. "I'm not sure that I'm fit for any sort of ministry, and I may find the winter in England trying to find out. I was at school in England, you know."

Ellen confessed that she had not known that.

"Yes; I suppose that's what made me seem 'so Englishy' the first day to Miss Lottie, as she called it. But I'm straight enough American as far as parentage goes. Do you think you will be in England-later?"

"I don't know. If poppa gets too homesick we will go back in the fall."

"Miss Kenton," said the young man, abruptly, "will you let me tell you how much I admire and revere your father?"

Tears came into her eyes and her throat swelled. "But you don't know," she begun; and then she stopped.

"I have been wanting to submit something to his judgment; but I've been afraid. I might seem to be fishing for his favor."

"Poppa wouldn't think anything that was unjust," said Ellen, gravely.

"Ah," Breckon laughed, "I suspect that I should rather have him unjust. I wish you'd tell me what he would think."

"But I don't know what it is," she protested, with a reflected smile.

"I was in hopes Miss Rasmith might have told you. Well, it is simply this, and you will see that I'm not quite the universal favorite she's been making you fancy me. There is a rift in my lute, a schism in my little society, which is so little that I could not have supposed there was enough of it to break in two. There are some who think their lecturer - for that's what I amount to - ought to be an older, if not a graver man. They are in the minority, but they're in the right, I'm afraid; and that's why I happen to be here telling you all this. It's a question of whether I ought to go back to New York or stay in London, where there's been a faint call for me." He saw the girl listening devoutly, with that flattered look which a serious girl cannot keep out of her face when a man confides a serious matter to her. "I might safely promise to be older, but could I keep my word if I promised to be graver? That's the point. If I were a Calvinist I might hold fast by faith, and fight it out with that; or if I were a Catholic I could cast myself upon the strength of the Church, and triumph in spite of temperament. Then it wouldn't matter whether I was grave or gay; it might be even better if I were gay. But," he went on, in terms which, doubtless, were not then for the first time formulated in his mind, "being merely the leader of a sort of forlorn hope in the Divine Goodness, perhaps I have no right to be so cheerful."

The note of a sad irony in his words appealed to such indignation for him in Ellen as she never felt for herself. But she only said, "I don't believe Poppa could take that in the wrong way if you told him."

Breckon stared. "Yes your father! What would he say?"

"I can't tell you. But I'm sure he would know what you meant."

"And you," he pursued, "what should YOU say?"

"I? I never thought about such a thing. You mustn't ask me, if you're serious; and if you're not -"

"But I am; I am deeply serious. I would like, to know how the case strikes you. I shall be so grateful if you will tell me."

"I'm sorry I can't, Mr. Breckon. Why don't you ask poppa?"

"No, I see now I sha'n't be able. I feel too much, after telling you, as if I had been posing. The reality has gone out of it all. And I'm ashamed."

"You mustn't be," she said, quietly; and she added, "I suppose it would be like a kind of defeat if you didn't go back?"

"I shouldn't care for the appearance of defeat," he said, courageously. "The great question is, whether somebody else wouldn't be of more use in my place."

"Nobody could be," said she, in a sort of impassioned absence, and then coming to herself, "I mean, they wouldn't think so, I don't believe."

"Then you advise -"

"No, no! I can't; I don't. I'm not fit to have an opinion about such a thing; it would be crazy. But poppa -"

They were at the door of the gangway, and she slipped within and left him. His nerves tingled, and there was a glow in his breast. It was sweet to have surprised that praise from her, though he could not have said why he should value the praise or a girl of her open ignorance and inexperience in everything that would have qualified her to judge him. But he found himself valuing it supremely, and wonderingly wishing to be worthy of it.

XVII

Ellen discovered her father with a book in a distant corner of the dining-saloon, which he preferred to the deck or the library for his reading, in such intervals as the stewards, laying and cleaning the tables, left him unmolested in it. She advanced precipitately upon him, and stood before him in an excitement which, though he lifted his dazed eyes to it from his page, he was not entirely aware of till afterwards. Then he realized that her cheeks were full of color, and her eyes of light, and that she panted as if she had been running when she spoke.

"Poppa," she said, "there is something that Mr. Breckon wants to speak to you - to ask you about. He has asked me, but I want you to see him, for I think he had better tell you himself."

While he still stared at her she was as suddenly gone as she had come, and he remained with his book, which the meaning had as suddenly left. There was no meaning in her words, except as he put it into them, and after he had got it in he struggled with it in a sort of perfunctory incredulity. It was not impossible; it chiefly seemed so because it seemed too good to be true; and the more he pondered it the more possible, if not probable, it became. He could not be safe with it till he had submitted it to his wife; and he went to her while he was sure of repeating Ellen's words without varying from them a syllable.

To his astonishment, Mrs. Kenton was instantly convinced. "Why, of course," she said, "it can't possibly mean anything else. Why should it be so very surprising? The time hasn't been very long, but they've been together almost every moment; and he was taken with her from the very beginning - I could see that. Put on your other coat," she said, as she dusted the collar of the coat the judge was wearing. "He'll be looking you up, at once. I can't say that it's unexpected," and she claimed a prescience in the matter which all her words had hitherto denied.

Kenton did not notice her inconsistency. "If it were not so exactly what I wished," he said, "I don't know that I should be surprised at it myself. Sarah, if I had been trying to imagine any one for Ellen, I couldn't have dreamed of a person better suited to her than this young man. He's everything that I could wish him to be. I've seen the pleasure and comfort she took in his way from the first moment. He seemed to make her forget - Do you suppose she has forgotten that miserable wretch Do you think -"

"If she hadn't, could she be letting him come to speak to you? I don't believe she ever really cared for Bittridge - or not after he began flirting with Mrs. Uphill." She had no shrinking from the names which Kenton avoided with disgust. "The only question for you is to consider what you shall say to Mr. Breckon."

"Say to him? Why, of course, if Ellen has made up her mind, there's only one thing I can say."

"Indeed there is! He ought to know all about that disgusting Bittridge business, and you have got to tell him."

"Sarah, I couldn't. It is too humiliating. How would it do to refer him to - You could manage that part so much better. I don't see how I could keep it from seeming an indelicate betrayal of the poor child -"

"Perhaps she's told him herself," Mrs. Kenton provisionally suggested.

The judge eagerly caught at the notion. "Do you think so? It would be like her! Ellen would wish him to know everything."

He stopped, and his wife could see that he was trembling with excitement. "We must find out. I will speak to Ellen -"

"And - you don't think I'd better have the talk with him first?"

"Certainly not!"

"Why, Rufus! You were not going to look him up?"

"No," he hesitated; but she could see that some such thing had been on his mind.

"Surely," she said, "you must be crazy!" But she had not the heart to blight his joy with sarcasm, and perhaps no sarcasm would have blighted it.

"I merely wondered what I had better say in case he spoke to me before you saw Ellen - that's all. Sarah! I couldn't have believed that anything could please me so much. But it does seem as if it were the assurance of Ellen's happiness; and she has deserved it, poor child! If ever there was a dutiful and loving daughter - at least before that wretched affair - she was one."

"She has been a good girl," Mrs. Kenton stoically admitted.

"And they are very well matched. Ellen is a cultivated woman. He never could have cause to blush for her, either her mind or her manners, in any circle of society; she would do him credit under any and all circumstances. If it were Lottie -"

"Lottie is all right," said her mother, in resentment of his preference; but she could not help smiling at it. "Don't you be foolish about Ellen. I approve of Mr. Breckon as much as you do. But it's her prettiness and sweetness that's taken his fancy, and not her wisdom, if she's got him."

"If she's got him?"

"Well, you know what I mean. I'm not saying she hasn't. Dear knows, I don't want to! I feel just as you do about it. I think it's the greatest piece of good fortune, coming on top of all our trouble with her. I couldn't have imagined such a thing."

He was instantly appeased. "Are you going to speak with Ellen" he radiantly inquired.

"I will see. There's no especial hurry, is there?"

"Only, if he should happen to meet me -"

"You can keep out of his way, I reckon. Or You can put him off, somehow."

"Yes," Kenton returned, doubtfully. "Don't," he added, "be too blunt with Ellen. You know she didn't say anything explicit to me."

"I think I will know how to manage, Mr. Kenton."

"Yes, of course, Sarah. I'm not saying that."

Breckon did not apparently try to find the judge before lunch, and at table he did not seem especially devoted to Ellen in her father's jealous eyes. He joked Lottie, and exchanged those passages or repartee with her in which she did not mind using a bludgeon when she had not a rapier at hand; it is doubtful if she was very sensible of the difference. Ellen sat by in passive content, smiling now and then, and Boyne carried on a dignified conversation with Mr. Pogis, whom he had asked to lunch at his table, and who listened with one ear to the vigorous retorts of Lottie in her combat with Breckon.

The judge witnessed it all with a grave displeasure, more and more painfully apparent to his wife. She could see the impatience, the gathering misgiving, in his face, and she perceived that she must not let this come to conscious dissatisfaction with Breckon; she knew her husband capable of indignation with trifling which would complicate the situation, if it came to that. She decided to speak with Ellen as soon as possible, and she meant to follow her to her state-room when they left the table. But fate assorted the pieces in the game differently. Boyne walked over to the place where Miss Rasmith was sitting with her mother; Lottie and Mr. Pogis went off to practise duets together, terrible, four-handed torments under which the piano presently clamored; and Ellen stood for a moment talked to by Mr. Breckon, who challenged her then for a walk on deck, and with whom she went away smiling.

Mrs. Kenton appealed with the reflection of the girl's happiness in her face to the frowning censure in her husband's; but Kenton spoke first. "What does he mean?" he demanded, darkly. "If he is making a fool of her he'll find that that game can't be played twice, with impunity. Sarah, I believe I should choke him."

"Mr. Kenton!" she gasped, and she trembled in fear of him, even while she kept herself with difficulty from shaking him for his folly. "Don't say such a thing! Can't you see that they want to talk it over? If he hasn't spoken to you it's because he wants to know how you took what she said." Seeing the effect of these arguments, she pursued: "Will you never have any sense? I will speak to Ellen the very minute I get her alone, and you have just got to wait. Don't you suppose it's hard for me, too? Have I got nothing to bear?"

Kenton went silently back to his book, which he took with him to the reading-room, where from time to time his wife came to him and reported that Ellen and Breckon were still walking up and down together, or that they were sitting down talking, or were forward, looking over at the prow, or were watching the deck-passengers dancing. Her husband received her successive advices with relaxing interest, and when she had brought the last she was aware that the affair was entirely in her hands with all the responsibility. After the gay parting between Ellen and Breckon, which took place late in the afternoon, she suffered an interval to elapse before she followed the girl down to her state-room. She found her lying in her berth, with shining eyes and glad, red cheeks; she was smiling to herself.

"That is right, Ellen," her mother said. "You need rest after your long tramp."

"I'm not tired. We were sitting down a good deal. I didn't think how late it was. I'm ever so much better. Where's Lottie?"

"Off somewhere with that young Englishman," said Mrs. Kenton, as if that were of no sort of consequence. "Ellen," she added, abruptly, trying within a tremulous smile to hide her eagerness, "what is this that Mr. Breckon wants to talk with your father about?"

"Mr. Breckon? With poppa?"

"Yes, certainly. You told him this morning that Mr. Breckon -"

"Oh! Oh yes!" said Ellen, as if recollecting something that had slipped her mind. "He wants poppa to advise him whether to go back to his congregation in New York or not."

Mrs. Kenton sat in the corner of the sofa next the door, looking into the girl's face on the pillow as she lay with her arms under her head. Tears of defeat and shame came into her eyes, and she could not see the girl's light nonchalance in adding:

"But he hasn't got up his courage yet. He thinks he'll ask him after dinner. He says he doesn't want poppa to think he's posing. I don't know what he means."

Mrs. Kenton did not speak at once. Her bitterest mortification was not for herself, but for the simple and tender father-soul which had been so tried already. She did not know how he would bear it, the disappointment, and the cruel hurt to his pride. But she wanted to fall on her knees in thankfulness that he had betrayed himself only to her.

She started in sudden alarm with the thought. "Where is he now - Mr. Breckon?"

"He's gone with Boyne down into the baggage-room."

Mrs. Kenton sank back in her corner, aware now that she would not have had the strength to go to her husband even to save him from the awful disgrace of giving himself away to Breckon. "And was that all?" she faltered.

"All?"

"That he wanted to speak to your father about?"

She must make irrefragably sure, for Kenton's sake, that she was not misunderstanding.

"Why, of course! What else? Why, momma! what are you crying about?"

"I'm not crying, child. Just some foolishness of your father's. He understood - he thought -" Mrs. Kenton began to laugh hysterically. "But you know how ridiculous he is; and he supposed - No, I won't tell you!"

It was not necessary. The girl's mind, perhaps because it was imbued already with the subject, had possessed itself of what filled her mother's. She dropped from the elbow on which she had lifted herself, and turned her face into the pillow, with a long wail of shame.

XVIII

Mrs. Kenton's difficulties in setting her husband right were indefinitely heightened by the suspicion that the most unsuspicious of men fell into concerning Breckon. Did Breckon suppose that the matter could be turned off in that way? he stupidly demanded; and when he was extricated from this error by his wife's representation that Breckon had not changed at all, but had never told Ellen that he wished to speak with him of anything but his returning to his society, Kenton still could not accept the fact. He would have contended that at least the other matter must have been in Breckon's mind; and when he was beaten from this position, and convinced that the meaning they had taken from Ellen's words had never been in any mind but their own, he fell into humiliation so abject that he could hide it only by the hauteur with which he carried himself towards Breckon when they met at dinner. He would scarcely speak to the young man; Ellen did not come to the table; Lottie and Boyne and their friend Mr. Pogis were dining with the Rasmiths, and Mrs. Kenton had to be, as she felt, cringingly kind to Breckon in explaining just the sort of temporary headache that kept her eldest daughter away. He was more than ordinarily sympathetic and polite, but he was manifestly bewildered by Kenton's behavior. He refused an hilarious invitation from Mrs. Rasmith, when he rose from table, to stop and have his coffee with her on his way out of the saloon. His old adorer explained that she had ordered a small bottle of champagne in honor of its being the night before they were to get into Boulogne, and that he ought to sit down and help her keep the young people straight. Julia, she brokenly syllabled, with the gay beverage bubbling back into her throat, was not the least use; she was worse than any. Julia did not look it, in the demure regard which she bent upon her amusing mother, and Breckon persisted in refusing. He said he thought he might safely leave them to Boyne, and Mrs. Rasmith said into her handkerchief, "Oh yes! Boyne!" and pressed Boyne's sleeve with her knobbed and jewelled fingers.

It was evident where most of the small bottle had gone, but Breckon was none the cheerfuller for the spectacle of Mrs. Rasmith. He could not have a moment's doubt as to the sort of work he had been doing in New York if she were an effect of it, and he turned his mind from the sad certainty back to the more important inquiry as to what offence his wish to advise with Judge Kenton could have conveyed. Ellen had told him in the afternoon that she had spoken with her father about it, and she had not intimated any displeasure or reluctance on him; but apparently he had decided not to suffer himself to be approached.

It might be as well. Breckon had not been able to convince himself that his proposal to consult Judge Kenton was not a pose. He had flashes of owning that it was contemplated merely as a means of ingratiating himself with Ellen. Now, as he found his way up and down among the empty steamer-chairs, he was aware, at the bottom of his heart, of not caring in the least for Judge Kenton's repellent bearing, except as it possibly, or impossibly, reflected some mood of hers. He could not make out her not coming to dinner; the headache was clearly an excuse; for some reason she did not wish to see him, he argued, with the egotism of his condition.

The logic of his conclusion was strengthened at breakfast by her continued absence; and this time Mrs. Kenton made no apologies for her. The judge was a shade less severe; or else Breckon did not put himself so much in the way to be withheld as he had the night before. Boyne and Lottie carried on a sort of muted scrap, unrebuked by their mother, who seemed too much distracted in some tacit trouble to mind them. From time to time Breckon found her eyes dwelling upon him wonderingly, entreatingly; she dropped them, if she caught his, and colored.

In the afternoon it was early evident that they were approaching Boulogne. The hatch was opened and the sailors began getting up the baggage of the passengers who were going to disembark. It seemed a long time for everybody till the steamer got in; those going ashore sat on their hand-baggage for an hour before the tug came up to take, them off. Mr. Pogis was among them; he had begun in the forenoon to mark the approaching separation between Lottie and himself by intervals of unmistakable withdrawal. Another girl might have cared, but Lottie did not care, for her failure to get a rise out of him by her mockingly varied "Oh, I say!" and "Well, rather!" In the growth of his dignified reserve Mr. Pogis was indifferent to jeers. By whatever tradition of what would or would not do he was controlled in relinquishing her acquaintance, or whether it was in obedience to some imperative ideal, or some fearful domestic influence subtly making itself felt from the coasts of his native island, or some fine despair of equalling the imagined grandeur of Lottie's social state in Tuskingum by anything he could show her in England, it was certain that he was ending with Lottie then and there. At the same time he was carefully defining himself from the Rasmiths, with whom he must land. He had his state-room things put at an appreciable distance, where he did not escape a final stab from Lottie.

"Oh, do give me a rose out of that," she entreated, in travestied imploring, as he stood looking at a withered bouquet which the steward had brought up with his rugs.

"I'm takin' it home," he explained, coldly.

"And I want to take a rose back to New York. I want to give it to a friend of mine there."

Mr. Pogis hesitated. Then he asked, "A man?" "Well, rather!" said Lottie.

He answered nothing, but looked definitively down at the flowers in his hand.

"Oh, I say!" Lottie exulted.

Boyne remained fixed in fealty to the Rasmiths, with whom Breckon was also talking as Mrs. Kenton came up with the judge. She explained how sorry her daughter Ellen was at not being able to say goodbye; she was still not at all well; and the ladies received her excuses with polite patience. Mrs. Rasmith said she did not know what they should do without Boyne, and Miss Rasmith put her arm across his shoulders and pulled him up to her, and implored, "Oh, give him to me, Mrs. Kenton!"

Boyne stole an ashamed look at his mother, and his father said, with an unbending to Breckon which must have been the effect of severe expostulation from Mrs. Kenton, "I suppose you and the ladies will go to Paris together."

"Why, no," Breckon said, and he added, with mounting confusion, "I - I had arranged to keep on to Rotterdam. I was going to mention it."

"Keep on to Rotterdam!" Mrs. Rasmith's eyes expressed the greatest astonishment.

"Why, of course, mother!" said her daughter. "Don't you know? Boyne told us."

Boyne, after their parting, seized the first chance of assuring his mother that he had not told Miss Rasmith that, for he had not known it, and he went so far in her condemnation to wonder how she could say such a thing. His mother said it was not very nice, and then suggested that perhaps she had heard it from some one else, and thought it was he. She acquitted him of complicity with Miss Rasmith in forbearing to contradict her; and it seemed to her a fitting time to find out from Boyne what she honestly could about the relation of the Rasmiths to Mr. Breckon. It was very little beyond their supposition, which every one else had shared, that he was going to land with them at Boulogne, and he must have changed his mind very suddenly. Boyne had not heard the Rasmiths speak of it. Miss Rasmith never spoke of Mr. Breckon at all; but she seemed to want to talk of Ellen; she was always asking about her, and what was the matter with her, and how long she had been sick.

"Boyne," said his mother, with a pang, "you didn't tell her anything about Ellen?"

"Momma!" said the boy, in such evident abhorrence of the idea that she rested tranquil concerning it. She paid little attention to what Boyne told her otherwise of the Rasmiths. Her own horizon were so limited that she could not have brought home to herself within them that wandering life the Rasmiths led from climate to climate and sensation to sensation, with no stay so long as the annually made in New York, where they sometimes passed months enough to establish themselves in giving and taking tea in a circle of kindred nomads. She conjectured as ignorantly as Boyne himself that they were very rich, and it would not have enlightened her to know that the mother was the widow of a California politician, whom she had married in the sort of middle period following upon her less mortuary survival of Miss Rasmith's father, whose name was not Rasmith.

What Mrs. Kenton divined was that they had wanted to get Breckon, and that so far as concerned her own interest in him they had wanted to get him away from Ellen. In her innermost self-confidences she did not permit herself the notion that Ellen had any right to him; but still it was a relief to have them off the ship, and to have him left. Of all the witnesses of the fact, she alone did not find it awkward. Breckon himself found it very awkward. He did not wish to be with the Rasmiths, but he found it uncomfortable not being with them, under the circumstances, and he followed them ashore in tingling reveries of explanation and apology. He had certainly meant to get off at Boulogne, and when he had suddenly and tardily made up his mind to keep on to Rotterdam, he had meant to tell them as soon as he had the labels on his baggage changed. He had not meant to tell them why he had changed his mind, and he did not tell them now in these tingling reveries. He did not own the reason in his secret thoughts, for it no longer seemed a reason; it no longer seemed a cause. He knew what the Rasmiths would think; but he could easily make that right with his conscience, at least, by parting with the Kentons at Rotterdam, and leaving them to find their unconducted way to any point they chose beyond. He separated himself uncomfortably from them when the tender had put off with her passengers and the ship had got under way again, and went to the smoking-room, while the judge returned to his book and Mrs. Kenton abandoned Lottie to her own devices, and took Boyne aside for her apparently fruitless inquiries.

They were not really so fruitless but that at the end of them she could go with due authority to look up her husband. She gently took his book from him and shut it up. "Now, Mr. Kenton," she began, "if you don't go right straight and find Mr. Breckon and talk with him, I - I don't know what I will do. You must talk to him -"

"About Ellen?" the judge frowned.

"No, certainly not. Talk with him about anything that interests you. Be pleasant to him. Can't you see that he's going on to Rotterdam on our account?"

"Then I wish he wasn't. There's no use in it."

"No matter! It's polite in him, and I want you to show him that you appreciate it."

"Now see here, Sarah," said the judge, "if you want him shown that we appreciate his politeness why don't you do it yourself?"

"I? Because it would look as if you were afraid to. It would look as if we meant something by it."

"Well, I am afraid; and that's just what I'm afraid of. I declare, my heart comes into my mouth whenever I think what an escape we had. I think of it whenever I look at him, and I couldn't talk to him without having that in my mind all the time. No, women can manage those things better. If you believe he is going along on our account, so as to help us see Holland, and to keep us from getting into scrapes, you're the one to make it up to him. I don't care what you say to show him our gratitude. I reckon we will get into all sorts of trouble if we're left to ourselves. But if you think he's stayed because he wants to be with Ellen, and -"

"Oh, I don't KNOW what I think! And that's silly I can't talk to him. I'm afraid it'll seem as if we wanted to flatter him, and goodness knows we don't want to. Or, yes, we do! I'd give anything if it was true. Rufus, do you suppose he did stay on her account? My, oh my! If I could only think so! Wouldn't it be the best thing in the world for the poor child, and for all of us? I never saw anybody that I liked so much. But it's too good to be true."

"He's a nice fellow, but I don't think he's any too good for Ellen."

"I'm not saying he is. The great thing is that he's good enough, and gracious knows what will happen if she meets some other worthless fellow, and gets befooled with him! Or if she doesn't take a fancy to some one, and goes back to Tuskingum without seeing any one else she likes, there is that awful wretch, and when she hears what Dick did to him - she's just wrong-headed enough to take up with him again to make amends to him. Oh, dear oh, dear! I know Lottie will let it out to her yet!"

The judge began threateningly, "You tell Lottie from me -"

"What?" said the girl herself, who had seen her father and mother talking together in a remote corner of the music-room and had stolen light-footedly upon them just at this moment.

"Lottie, child," said her mother, undismayed at Lottie's arrival in her larger anxiety, "I wish you would try and be agreeable to Mr. Breckon. Now that he's going on with us to Holland, I don't want him to think we're avoiding him."

"Why?"

"Oh, because."

"Because you want to get him for Ellen?"

"Don't be impudent," said her father. "You do as your mother bids you."

"Be agreeable to that old Breckon? I think I see myself! I'd sooner read! I'm going to get a book now." She left them as abruptly as she had come upon them, and ran across to the bookcase, where she remained two stepping and peering through the glass doors at the literature within, in unaccustomed question concerning it.

"She's a case," said the judge, looking at her not only with relenting, but with the pride in her sufficiency for all the exigencies of life which he could not feel in Ellen. "She can take care of herself."

"Oh yes," Mrs. Kenton sadly assented, "I don't think anybody will ever make a fool of Lottie."

"It's a great deal more likely to be the other way," her father suggested.

"I think Lottie is conscientious," Mrs. Kenton protested. "She wouldn't really fool with a man."

"No, she's a good girl," the judge owned.

"It's girls like Ellen who make the trouble and the care. They are too good, and you have to think some evil in this world. Well!" She rose and gave her husband back his book.

"Do you know where Boyne is?"

"No. Do you want him to be pleasant to Mr. Breckon?"

"Somebody has got to. But it would be ridiculous if nobody but Boyne was."

She did not find Boyne, after no very exhaustive search, and the boy was left to form his bearing towards Breckon on the behavior of the rest of his family. As this continued helplessly constrained both in his father and mother, and voluntarily repellent in Lottie, Boyne decided upon a blend of conduct which left Breckon in greater and greater doubt of his wisdom in keeping on to Rotterdam. There was no good reason which he would have been willing to give himself, from the beginning. It had been an impulse, suddenly coming upon him in the baggage-room where he had gone to get something out of his trunk, and where he had decided to have the label of his baggage changed from the original destination at Boulogne to the final port of the steamer's arrival. When this was once done he was sorry, but he was ashamed to have the label changed back. The most assignable motive for his act was his reluctance to go on to Paris with the Rasmiths, or rather with Mrs. Rasmith; for with her daughter, who was not a bad fellow, one could always manage. He was quite aware of being safely in his own hands against any design of Mrs. Rasmith's, but her machinations humiliated him for her; he hated to see her going through her manoeuvres, and he could not help grieving for her failures, with a sort of impersonal sympathy, all the more because he disliked her as little as he respected her.

The motive which he did not assign to himself was that which probably prevailed with him, though in the last analysis it was as selfish, no doubt, as the one he acknowledged. Ellen Kenton still piqued his curiosity, still touched his compassion. He had so far from exhausted his wish or his power to befriend her, to help her, that he had still a wholly unsatisfied longing to console her, especially when she drooped into that listless attitude she was apt to take, with her face fallen and her hands let lie, the back of one in the palm of the other, in her lap. It was possibly the vision of this following him to the baggage-room, when he went to open his trunk, that as much as anything decided him to have the label changed on his baggage, but he did not own it then, and still less did he own it now, when he found himself quite on his own hands for his pains.

He felt that for some reason the Kentons were all avoiding him. Ellen, indeed, did not take part, against him, unless negatively, for she had appeared neither at lunch nor at dinner as the vessel kept on its way after leaving Boulogne; and when he ventured to ask for her Mrs. Kenton answered with embarrassment that she was not feeling very well. He asked for her at lunch, but not at dinner, and when he had finished that meal he went on the promenade-deck, and walked forlornly up and down, feeling that he had been a fool.

Mrs. Kenton went below to her daughter's room, and found Ellen there on the sofa, with her book shut on her thumb at the place where the twilight had failed her.

"Ellen, dear," her mother said, "aren't you feeling well?"

"Yes, I'm well enough," said the girl, sensible of a leading in the question. "Why?"

"Oh, nothing. Only - only I can't make your father behave naturally with Mr. Breckon. He's got his mind so full of that mistake we both came so near making that he can't think of anything else. He's so sheepish about it that he can hardly speak to him or even look at him; and I must confess that I don't do much better. You know I don't like to put myself forward where your father is, and if I did, really I don't believe I could make up my mouth to say anything. I did want Lottie to be nice to him, but Lottie dislikes him so! And even Boyne - well, it wouldn't matter about Boyne, if he didn't seem to be carrying out a sort of family plan - Boyne barely answers him when he speaks to him. I don't know what he can think." Ellen was a good listener, and Mrs. Kenton, having begun, did not stop till she had emptied the bag. "I just know that he didn't get off at Boulogne because he wanted to stay on with us, and thought he could be useful to us at The Hague, and everywhere; and here we're acting as ungratefully! Why, we're not even commonly polite to him, and I know he feels it. I know that he's hurt."

Ellen rose and stood before the glass, into which he asked of her mother's reflected face, while she knotted a fallen coil of hair into its place, "Where is he?"

"I don't know. He went on deck somewhere."

Ellen put on her hat and pinned it, and put on her jacket and buttoned it. Then she started towards the door. Her mother made way for her, faltering, "What are you going to do, Ellen?"

"I am going to do right."

"Don't-catch cold!" her mother called after her figure vanishing down the corridor, but the warning couched in these terms had really no reference to the weather.

The girl's impulse was one of those effects of the weak will in her which were apt to leave her short of the fulfilment of a purpose. It carried her as her as the promenade, which she found empty, and she went and leaned upon the rail, and looked out over the sorrowful North Sea, which was washing darkly away towards where the gloomy sunset had been.

Steps from the other side of the ship approached, hesitated

towards her, and then arrested themselves. She looked round.

"Why, Miss Kenton!" said Breckon, stupidly.

"The sunset is over, isn't it?" she answered.

"The twilight isn't." Breckon stopped; then he asked, "Wouldn't you like to take a little walk?"

"Yes," she answered, and smiled fully upon him. He had never known before how radiant a smile she lead.

"Better have my arm. It's getting rather dark."

"Well." She put her hand on his arm and he felt it tremble there, while she palpitated, "We are all so glad you could go on to Rotterdam. My mother wanted me to tell you."

"Oh, don't speak of that," said Breckon, not very appositely. Presently he forced a laugh, in order to add, with lightness, "I was afraid perhaps I had given you all some reason to regret it!"

She said, "I was afraid you would think that - or momma was - and I couldn't bear to have you."

"Well, then, I won't."

XIX

Breckon had answered with gayety, but his happiness was something beyond gayety. He had really felt the exclusion from the Kentons in which he had passed the day, and he had felt it the more painfully because he liked them all. It may be owned that he liked Ellen best from the beginning, and now he liked her better than ever, but even in the day's exile he had not ceased to like each of them. They were, in their family affection, as lovable as that sort of selfishness can make people. They were very united and good to one another. Lottie herself, except in her most lurid moments, was good to her brother and sister, and almost invariably kind to her parents. She would not, Breckon saw, have brooked much meddling with her flirtations from them, but as they did not offer to meddle, she had no occasion to grumble on that score. She grumbled when they asked her to do things for Ellen, but she did them, and though she never did them without grumbling, she sometimes did them without being asked. She was really very watchful of Ellen when it would least have been expected, and sometimes she was sweet. She never was sweet with Boyne, but she was often his friend, though this did not keep her from turning upon him at the first chance to give him a little dig, or a large one, for that matter. As for Boyne, he was a mass of helpless sweetness, though he did not know it, and sometimes took himself for an iceberg when he was merely an ice-cream of heroic mould. He was as helplessly sweet with Lottie as with any one, and if he suffered keenly from her treacheries, and seized every occasion to repay them in kind, it was clearly a matter of conscience with him, and always for the good. Their

William Dean Howells

father and mother treated their squabbles very wisely, Breckon thought. They ignored them as much as possible, and they recognized them without attempting to do that justice between them which would have rankled in both their breasts.

To a spectator who had been critical at first, Mr. and Mrs. Kenton seemed an exemplary father and mother with Ellen as well as with their other children. It is easy to be exemplary with a sick girl, but they increasingly affected Breckon as exemplary with Ellen. He fancied that they acted upon each other beneficially towards her. At first he had foreboded some tiresome boasting from the father's tenderness, and some weak indulgence of the daughter's whims from her mother; but there was either never any ground for this, or else Mrs. Kenton, in keeping her husband from boasting, had been obliged in mere consistency to set a guard upon her own fondness.

It was not that. Ellen, he was more and more decided, would have abused the weakness of either; if there was anything more angelic than her patience, it was her wish to be a comfort to them, and, between the caprices of her invalidism, to be a service. It was pathetic to see her remembering to do things for them which Boyne and Lottie had forgotten, or plainly shirked doing, and to keep the fact out of sight. She really kept it out of sight with them, and if she did not hide it from so close an observer as Breckon, that was more his fault than hers. When her father first launched out in her praise, or the praise of her reading, the young man had dreaded a rustic prig; yet she had never been a prig, but simply glad of what book she had known, and meekly submissive to his knowledge if not his taste. He owned that she had a right to her taste, which he found almost always good, and accounted for as instinctive in the absence of an imaginable culture in her imaginable ambient. So far as he had glimpses of this, he found it so different from anything he had known that the modest adequacy of Mrs. Kenton in the political experiences of modern Europe, as well as the clear judgments of Kenton himself in matters sometimes beyond Breekon himself, mystified him no less than Ellen's taste.

Even with the growth of his respect for their intelligence and his love of their kindliness, he had not been able to keep a certain patronage from mingling, and it was not till they evinced not only entire ability, but an apparent wish to get on without his approval, without his acquaintance even, that he had conceived a just sense of them. The like is apt to happen with the best of us, when we are also the finest, and Breckon was not singular in coming to a due consciousness of something valuable only in the hour of its loss. He did not know that the loss was only apparent. He knew that he had made a distinct sacrifice for these people, and that, when he had prepared himself to befriend them little short of self-devotion, they showed themselves indifferent, and almost repellent. In the revulsion of feeling, when Ellen gave him her mother's message, and frankly offered him reparation on behalf of her whole family, he may have overdone his gratitude, but he did not overdo it to her perception. They walked up and down the promenade of the Amstel, in the watery North Sea moon, while bells after bells noted the hour unheeded, and when they parted for the night it was with an involuntary pressure of hands, from which she suddenly pulled hers, and ran down the corridor of her state-room and Lottie's.

He stood watching the narrow space in which she had vanished, and thinking how gentle she was, and how she had contrived somehow to make him feel that now it was she who had been consoling him, and trying to interest him and amuse him. He had not realized that before; he had been used to interesting and amusing her, but he could not resent it; he could not resent the implication of superiority, if such a thing were possible, which her kindness conveyed. The question with Breckon was whether she had walked with him so long because she wished, in the hour, to make up as fully as possible for the day's neglect, or because she had liked to walk up and down with him. It was a question he found keeping itself poignantly, yet pleasantly, in his mind, after he had got into his berth under the solidly slumberous Boyne, and inclining now to one solution and now to the other, with a delicate oscillation that was charming.

The Amstel took her time to get into Rotterdam, and when her passengers had gone ashore the next forenoon the train that carried Breckon to The Hague in the same compartment with the Kentons was in no greater hurry. It arrived with a deliberation which kept it from carrying them on to Amsterdam before they knew it, and Mrs. Kenton had time to place such parts of the wars in the Rise of the Dutch Republic as she could attach to the names of the stations and the general features of the landscape. Boyne was occupied with improvements for the windmills and the canal-boats, which did not seem to him of the quality of the Michigan aerometers, or the craft with which he was familiar on the Hudson River and on the canal that passed through Tuskingum. Lottie, with respect to the canals, offered the frank observation that they smelt, and in recognizing a fact which travel almost universally ignores in Holland, she watched her chance of popping up the window between herself and Boyne, which Boyne put down with mounting rage. The agriculture which triumphed everywhere on the little half - acre plots lifted fifteen inches above the waters of the environing ditches, and the black and white cattle everywhere attesting the immemorial Dutch ideal of a cow, were what at first occupied Kenton, and he was tardily won from them to the question of fighting over a country like that. It was a concession to his wife's impassioned interest in the overthrow of the Spaniards in a landscape which had evidently not changed since. She said it was hard to realize that Holland was not still a republic, and she was not very patient with Breckon's defence of the monarchy on the ground that the young Queen was a very pretty girl.

"And she is only sixteen," Boyne urged.

"Then she is two years too old for you," said Lottie.

"No such thing!" Boyne retorted. "I was fifteen in June."

"Dear me! I should never have thought it," said his sister.

Ellen seemed hardly to look out of the window at anything directly, but when her father bade her see this thing and that, it seemed that she had seen it already. She said at last, with a quiet sigh, "I never want to go away."

She had been a little shy of Breckon the whole morning, and had kept him asking himself whether she was sorry she had walked so long with him the night before, or, having offered him due reparation for her family, she was again dropping him. Now and then he put her to the test by words explicitly directed at her, and she replied with the dreamy passivity which seemed her normal mood, and in which he could fancy himself half forgotten, or remembered with an effort.

In the midst of this doubt she surprised him - he reflected that she was always surprising him - by asking him how far it was from The Hague to the sea. He explained that The Hague was in the sea like all the rest of Holland, but that if she meant the shore, it was no distance at all. Then she said, vaguely, she wished they were going to the shore. Her father asked Breckon if there was not a hotel at the beach, and the young man tried to give him a notion of the splendors of the Kurhaus at Scheveningen; of Scheveningen itself he despaired of giving any just notion.

"Then we can go there," said the judge, ignoring Ellen, in his decision, as if she had nothing to do with it.

Lottie interposed a vivid preference for The Hague. She had, she said, had enough of the sea for one while, and did not want to look at it again till they sailed for home. Boyne turned to his father as if a good deal shaken by this reasoning, and it was Mrs. Kenton who carried the day for going first to a hotel in The Hague and prospecting from there in the direction of Scheveningen; Boyne and his father could go down to the shore and see which they liked best.

"I don't see what that has to do with me," said Lottie. No one was alarmed by her announcement that if she did not like Scheveningen she should stay at The Hague, whatever the rest did; in the event fortune favored her going with her family.

The hotel in The Hague was very pleasant, with a garden behind it, where a companionable cat had found a dry spot, and where Lottie found the cat and made friends with it. But she said the hotel was full of Cook's tourists, whom she recognized, in spite of her lifelong ignorance of them, by a prescience derived from the conversation of Mr. Pogis, and from the instinct of a society woman, already rife in her. She found that she could not stay in a hotel with Cook's tourists, and she took her father's place in the exploring party which went down to the watering-place in the afternoon, on the top of a tram-car, under the leafy roof of the adorable avenue of trees which embowers the track to Scheveningen. She disputed Boyne's impressions of the Dutch people, whom he found looking more like Americans than any foreigners he had seen, and she snubbed Breckon from his supposed charge of the party. But after the start, when she declared that Ellen could not go, and that it was ridiculous for her to think of it, she was very good to her, and looked after her safety and comfort with a despotic devotion.

At the Kurhaus she promptly took the lead in choosing rooms, for she had no doubt of staying there after the first glance at the place, and she showed a practical sense in settling her family which at least her mother appreciated when they were installed the next day.

Mrs. Kenton could not make her husband admire Lottie's faculty so readily. "You think it would have been better for her to sit down with Ellen, on the sand and dream of the sea," she reproached him, with a tender resentment on behalf of Lottie. "Everybody can't dream."

"Yes, but I wish she didn't keep awake with such a din," said the judge. After all, he admired Lottie's judgment about the rooms, and he censured her with a sigh of relief from care as he sank back in the easy-chair fronting the window that looked out on the North Sea; Lottie had already made him appreciate the view till he was almost sick of it.

"What is the matter?" said Mrs. Kenton, sharply. "Do you want to be in Tuskingum? I suppose you would rather be looking into Richard's back-yard."

"No," said the judge, mildly, "this is very nice."

"It will do Ellen good, every minute. I don't care how much she sits on the sands and dream. I'll love to see her."

The sitting on the sand was a survival of Mr. Kenton's preoccupations of the sea-side. As a mater of fact, Ellen was at that moment sitting in one of the hooked wicker arm-chairs which were scattered over the whole vast beach like a growth of monstrous mushrooms, and, confronting her in cosey proximity, Breckon sat equally hidden in another windstuhl. Her father and her mother were able to keep them placed, among the multitude of windstuhls, by the presence of Lottie, who hovered near them, and, with Boyne, fended off the demure, wicked-looking little Scheveningen girls. On a smaller scale these were exactly like their demure, wicked-looking Scheveningen mothers, and they approached with knitting in their hands, and with large stones folded in their aprons, which they had pilfered from the mole, and were trying to sell for footstools. The windstuhl men and they were enemies, and when Breckon bribed them to go away, the windstuhl men chased them, and the little girls ran, making mouths at Boyne over their shoulders. He scorned to notice them; but he was obliged to report the misconduct of Lottie, who began making eyes at the Dutch officers as soon as she could feel that Ellen was safely off her hands. She was the more exasperating and the more culpable to Boyne, because she had asked him to walk up the beach with her, and had then made the fraternal promenade a basis of operations against the Dutch military. She joined her parents in ignoring Boyne's complaints, and continued to take credit for all the pleasant facts of the situation; she patronized her family as much for the table d'hote at luncheon as for the comfort of their rooms. She was able to assure them that there was not a Cook's tourist in the hotel, where there seemed to be nearly every other kind of fellow-creature. At the end of the first week she had acquaintance of as many nationalities as she could reach in their native or acquired English, in all the stages of haughty toleration, vivid intimacy, and cold exhaustion. She had a faculty for getting through with people, or of ceasing to have any use for them, which was perhaps her best safeguard in her adventurous flirting; while the simple aliens were still in the full tide of fancied success, Lottie was sick of them all, and deep in an indiscriminate correspondence with her young men in Tuskingum.

The letters which she had invited from these while still in New York arrived with the first of those readdressed from the judge's London banker. She had more letters than all the rest of the family together, and counted a half-dozen against a poor two for her sister. Mrs. Kenton cared nothing about Lottie's letters, but she was silently uneasy about the two that Ellen carelessly took. She wondered who could be writing to Ellen, especially in a cover bearing a handwriting altogether strange to her.

"It isn't from Bittridge, at any rate," she said to her husband, in the speculation which she made him share. "I am always dreading to have her find out what Richard did. It would spoil everything, I'm afraid, and now everything is going so well. I do wish Richard hadn't, though, of course, he did it for the best. Who do you think has been writing to her?"

"Why don't you ask her?"

"I suppose she will tell me after a while. I don't like to seem to be following her up. One was from Bessie Pearl, I think."

Ellen did not speak of her letters to her mother, and after

waiting a day or two, Mrs. Kenton could not refrain from asking her.

"Oh, I forgot," said Ellen. "I haven't read them yet."

"Haven't read them!" said Mrs. Kenton. Then, after reflection, she added, "You are a strange girl, Ellen," and did not venture to say more.

"I suppose I thought I should have to answer them, and that made me careless. But I will read them." Her mother was silent, and presently Ellen added: "I hate to think of the past. Don't you, momma?"

"It is certainly very pleasant here," said Mrs. Kenton, cautiously. "You're enjoying yourself - I mean, you seem to be getting so much stronger."

"Why, momma, why do you talk as if I had been sick?" Ellen asked.

"I mean you're so much interested."

"Don't I go about everywhere, like anybody?" Ellen pursued, ignoring her explanation.

"Yes, you certainly do. Mr. Breckon seems to like going about."

Ellen did not respond to the suggestion except to say: "We go into all sorts of places. This morning we went up on that schooner that's drawn up on the beach, and the old man who was there was very pleasant. I thought it was a wreck, but Mr. Breckon says they are always drawing their ships that way up on the sand. The old man was patching some of the wood-work, and he told Mr. Breckon - he can speak a little Dutch – that they were going to drag her down to the water and go fishing as soon as he was done. He seemed to think we were brother and sister." She flushed a little, and then she said: "I believe I like the dunes as well as anything. Sometimes when those curious cold breaths come in from the sea we climb up in the little hollows on the other side and sit there out of the draft. Everybody seems to do it."

Apparently Ellen was submitting the propriety of the fact to her mother, who said: "Yes, it seems to be quite the same as it is at home. I always supposed that it was different with young people here. There is certainly no harm in it."

Ellen went on, irrelevantly. "I like to go and look at the Scheveningen women mending the nets on the sand back of the dunes. They have such good gossiping times. They shouted to us last evening, and then laughed when they saw us watching them. When they got through their work they got up and stamped off so strong, with their bare, red arms folded into their aprons, and their skirts sticking out so stiff. Yes, I should like to be like them."

"You, Ellen!"

"Yes; why not?"

Mrs. Kenton found nothing better to answer than,

"They were very material looking."

"They are very happy looking. They live in the present. That is what I should like: living in the present, and not looking backwards or forwards. After all, the present is the only life we've got, isn't it?"

"I suppose you may say it is," Mrs. Kenton admitted, not knowing just where the talk was leading, but dreading to interrupt it.

"But that isn't the Scheveningen woman's only ideal. Their other ideal is to keep the place clean. Saturday afternoon they were all out scrubbing the brick sidewalks, and clear into the middle of the street. We were almost ashamed to walk over the nice bricks, and we picked out as many dirty places as we could find."

Ellen laughed, with a light-hearted gayety that was very strange to her, and Mrs. Kenton, as she afterwards told her husband, did not know what to think.

"I couldn't help wondering," she said, "whether the poor child would have liked to keep on living in the present a month ago."

"Well, I'm glad you didn't say so," the judge answered.

XX

From the easy conquest of the men who looked at her Lottie proceeded to the subjection of the women. It would have been more difficult to put these down, if the process had not been so largely, so almost entirely subjective. As it was, Lottie exchanged snubs with many ladies of the continental nationalities who were never aware of having offered or received offence. In some cases, when they fearlessly ventured to speak with her, they behaved very amiable, and seemed to find her conduct sufficiently gracious in return. In fact, she was approachable enough, and had no shame, before Boyne, in dismounting from the high horse which she rode when alone with him, and meeting these ladies on foot, at least half-way. She made several of them acquainted with her mother, who, after a timorous reticence, found them very conversable, with a range of topics, however, that shocked her American sense of decorum. One Dutch lady talked with such manly freedom, and with such untrammelled intimacy, that she was obliged to send Boyne and Lottie about their business, upon an excuse that was not apparent to the Dutch lady. She only complimented Mrs. Kenton upon her children and their devotion to each other, and when she learned that Ellen was also her daughter, ventured the surmise she was not long married.

"It isn't her husband," Mrs. Kenton explained, with inward trouble. "It's just a gentleman that came over with us," and she went with her trouble to her own husband as soon as she could.

"I'm afraid it isn't the custom to go around alone with young men as much as Ellen thinks," she suggested.

"He ought to know," said the judge. "I don't suppose he would if it wasn't."

"That is true," Mrs. Kenton owned, and for the time she put her misgivings away.

"So long as we do nothing wrong," the judge decided, "I don't see why we should not keep to our own customs."

"Lottie says they're not ours, in New York."

"Well, we are not in New York now."

They had neither of them the heart to interfere with Ellen's happiness, for, after all, Breckon was careful enough of the appearances, and it was only his being constantly with Ellen that suggested the Dutch lady's surmise. In fact, the range of their wanderings was not beyond the dunes, though once they went a little way on one of the neatly bricked country roads that led towards The Hague. As yet there had been no movement in any of the party to see the places that lie within such easy tram-reach of The Hague, and the hoarded interest of the past in their keeping. Ellen chose to dwell in the actualities which were an enlargement of her own present, and Lottie's active spirit found employment enough in the amusements at the Kurhaus. She shopped in the little bazars which make a Saratoga under the colonnades fronting two sides of the great space before the hotel, and she formed a critical and exacting taste in music from a constant attendance at the afternoon concerts; it is true that during the winter in New York she had cast forever behind her the unsophisticated ideals of Tuskingum in the art, so that from the first she was able to hold the famous orchestra that played in the Kurhaus concert-room up to the highest standard. She had no use for anybody who had any use for rag-time, and she was terribly severe with a young American, primarily of Boyne's acquaintance, who tried to make favor with her by asking about the latest coon-songs. She took the highest ethical ground with him about tickets in a charitable lottery which he had bought from the portier, but could not move him on the lower level which he occupied. He offered to give her the picture which was the chief prize, in case he won it, and she assured him beforehand that she should not take it. She warned Boyne against him, under threats of exposure to their mother, as not a good influence, but one afternoon, when the young Queen of Holland came to the concert with the queen-mother, Lottie cast her prejudices to the winds in accepting the places which the wicked fellow-countryman offered Boyne and herself, when they had failed to get any where they could see the queens, as the Dutch called them.

The hotel was draped with flags, and banked with flowers about the main entrance where the queens were to arrive, and the guests massed themselves in a dense lane for them to pass through. Lottie could not fail to be one of the foremost in this array, and she was able to decide, when the queens had passed, that the younger would not be considered a more than average pretty girl in America, and that she was not very well dressed. They had all stood within five feet of her, and Boyne had appropriated one of the prettiest of the pretty bends which the gracious young creature made to right and left, and had responded to it with an 'empressement' which he hoped had not been a sacrifice of his republican principles.

During the concert he sat with his eyes fixed upon the Queen where she sat in the royal box, with her mother and her ladies behind her, and wondered and blushed to wonder if she had noticed him when he bowed, or if his chivalric devotion in applauding her when the audience rose to receive her had been more apparent than that of others; whether it had seemed the heroic act of setting forth at the head of her armies, to beat back a German invasion, which it had essentially been, with his instantaneous return as victor, and the Queen's abdication and adoption of republican principles under conviction of his reasoning, and her idolized consecration as the first chief of the

Dutch republic. His cheeks glowed, and he quaked at heart lest Lottie should surprise his thoughts and expose them to that sarcastic acquaintance, who proved to be a medical student resting at Scheveningen from the winter's courses and clinics in, Vienna. He had already got on to many of Boyne's curves, and had sacrilegiously suggested the Queen of Holland when he found him feeding his fancy on the modern heroical romances; he advised him as an American adventurer to compete with the European princes paying court to her. So thin a barrier divided that malign intelligence from Boyne's most secret dreams that he could never feel quite safe from him, and yet he was always finding himself with him, now that he was separated from Miss Rasmith, and Mr. Breckon was taken up so much with Ellen. On the ship he could put many things before Mr. Breckon which must here perish in his breast, or suffer the blight of this Mr. Trannel's raillery. The student sat near the Kentons at table, and he was no more reverent of the judge's modest convictions than of Boyne's fantastic preoccupations. The worst of him was that you could not help liking him: he had a fascination which the boy felt while he dreaded him, and now and then he did something so pleasant that when he said something unpleasant you could hardly believe it.

At the end of the concert, when he rose and stood with all the rest, while the royal party left their box, and the orchestra played the Dutch national hymn, he said, in a loud whisper, to Boyne: "Now's your time, my boy! Hurry out and hand her into her carriage!"

Boyne fairly reeled at the words which translated a passage of the wild drama playing itself in his brain, and found little support in bidding his tormentor, "Shut up!" The retort, rude as it was, seemed insufficient, but Boyne tried in vain to think of something else. He tried to punish him by separating Lottie from him, but failed as signally in that. She went off with him, and sat in a windstuhl facing his the rest of the afternoon, with every effect of carrying on.

Boyne was helpless, with his mother against it, when he appealed to her to let him go and tell Lottie that she wanted her. Mrs. Kenton said that she saw no harm in it, that Ellen was sitting in like manner with Mr. Breckon.

"Mr. Breckon is very different, and Ellen knows how to behave," he urged, but his mother remained unmoved, or was too absent about something to take any interest in the matter. In fact, she was again unhappy about Ellen, though she put on such an air of being easy about her. Clearly, so far as her maternal surmise could fathom the case, Mr. Breckon was more and more interested in Ellen, and it was evident that the child was interested in him. The situation was everything that was acceptable to Mrs. Kenton, but she shuddered at the cloud which hung over it, and which might any moment involve it. Again and again she had made sure that Lottie had given Ellen no hint of Richard's ill-advised vengeance upon Bittridge; but it was not a thing that could be kept always, and the question was whether it could be kept till Ellen had accepted Mr. Breckon and married him. This was beyond the question of his asking her to do so, but it was so much more important that Mrs. Kenton was giving it her attention first, quite out of the order of time. Besides, she had every reason, as she felt, to count upon the event. Unless he was trifling with Ellen, far more wickedly than Bittridge, he was in love with her, and in Mrs. Kenton's simple experience and philosophy of life, being in love was briefly preliminary to marrying. If she went with her anxieties to her husband, she had first to reduce him from a buoyant optimism concerning the affair before she could get him to listen seriously. When this was accomplished he fell into such despair that she ended in lifting him up and supporting him with hopes that she did not feel herself. What they were both united in was the conviction that nothing so good could happen in the world, but they were equally united in the old American tradition that they must not lift a finger to secure this supreme good for their child.

It did not seem to them that leaving the young people constantly to themselves was doing this. They interfered with

Ellen now neither more nor less than they had interfered with her as to Bittridge, or than they would have interfered with her in the case of any one else. She was still to be left entirely to herself in such matters, and Mrs. Kenton would have kept even her thoughts off her if she could. She would have been very glad to give her mind wholly to the study of the great events which had long interested her here in their scene, but she felt that until the conquest of Mr. Breckon was secured beyond the hazard of Ellen's morbid defection at the supreme moment, she could not give her mind to the history of the Dutch republic.

"Don't bother me about Lottie, Boyne," she said. "I have enough to think of without your nonsense. If this Mr. Trannel is an American, that is all that is necessary. We are all Americans together, and I don't believe it will make remark, Lottie's sitting on the beach with him."

"I don't see how he's different from that Bittridge," said Boyne. "He doesn't care for anything; and he plays the banjo just like him."

Mrs. Kenton was too troubled to laugh. She said, with finality, "Lottie can take care of herself," and then she asked, "Boyne, do you know whom Ellen's letters were from?"

"One was from Bessie Pearl -"

"Yes, she showed me that. But you don't know who the other was from?"

"No; she didn't tell me. You know how close Ellen is."

"Yes," the mother sighed, "she is very odd."

Then she added, "Don't you let her know that I asked you about her letters."

"No," said Boyne. His audience was apparently at an end, but

William Dean Howells

he seemed still to have something on his mind. "Momma," he began afresh.

"Well?" she answered, a little impatiently.

"Nothing. Only I got to thinking, Is a person able to control their - their fancies?"

"Fancies about what?"

"Oh, I don't know. About falling in love." Boyne blushed.

"Why do you want to know? You musn't think about such things, a boy like you! It's a great pity that you ever knew anything about that Bittridge business. It's made you too bold. But it seems to have been meant to drag us down and humiliate us in every way."

"Well, I didn't try to know anything about it," Boyne retorted.

"No, that's true," his mother did him the justice to recognize. "Well, what is it you want to know?" Boyne was too hurt to answer at once, and his mother had to coax him a little. She did it sweetly, and apologized to him for saying what she had said. After all, he was the youngest, and her baby still. Her words and caresses took effect at last, and he stammered out, "Is everybody so, or is it only the Kentons that seem to be always putting - well, their affections - where it's perfectly useless?"

His mother pushed him from her. "Boyne, are you silly about that ridiculous old Miss Rasmith?"

"No!" Boyne shouted, savagely, "I'm NOT!"

"Who is it, then?"

"I sha'n't tell you!" Boyne said, and tears of rage and shame came into his eyes.

XXI

In his exile from his kindred, for it came practically to that, Boyne was able to add a fine gloom to the state which he commonly observed with himself when he was not giving way to his morbid fancies or his morbid fears, and breaking down in helpless subjection to the nearest member of his household. Lottie was so taken up with her student that she scarcely quarrelled with him any more, and they had no longer those moments of union in which they stood together against the world. His mother had cast him off, as he felt, very heartlessly, though it was really because she could not give his absurdities due thought in view of the hopeful seriousness of Ellen's affair, and Boyne was aware that his father at the best of times was ignorant of him when he was not impatient of him. These were not the best of times with Judge Kenton, and Boyne was not the first object of his impatience. In the last analysis he was living until he could get home, and so largely in the hope of this that his wife at times could scarcely keep him from taking some step that would decide the matter between Ellen and Breckon at once. They were tacitly agreed that they were waiting for nothing else, and, without making their agreement explicit, she was able to quell him by asking what he expected to do in case there was nothing between them? Was he going to take the child back to Tuskingum, which was the same as taking her back to Bittridge? it hurt her to confront him with this question, and she tried other devices for staying and appeasing him. She begged him now, seeing Boyne so forlorn, and hanging about the hotel alone, or moping over those ridiculous books of his, to go off with the boy somewhere and see the interesting places within such easy reach, like Leyden and Delft if he cared nothing for the place where William the Silent was shot, he ought to see the place that the Pilgrims started from. She had counted upon doing those places herself, with her husband, and it was in a sacrifice of her ideal that she now urged him to go with Boyne. But her preoccupation with Ellen's affair forbade her self-abandon to those high historical interests to which she urged his devotion. She might have gone with him and Boyne, but then she must have left the larger half of her divided mind with Ellen, not to speak of Lottie, who refused to be a party to any such excursion. Mrs. Kenton felt the disappointment and grieved at it, but not without hope of repairing it later, and she did not cease from entreating the judge to do what he could at once towards fulfilling the desires she postponed. Once she prevailed with him, and really got him and Boyne off for a day, but they came back early, with signs of having bored each other intolerably, and after that it was Boyne, as much as his father, who relucted from joint expeditions. Boyne did not so much object to going alone, and his father said it was best to let him, though his mother had her fears for her youngest. He spent a good deal of his time on the trams between Scheveningen and The Hague, and he was understood to have explored the capital pretty thoroughly. In fact, he did go about with a valet de place, whom he got at a cheap rate, and with whom he conversed upon the state of the country and its political affairs. The valet said that the only enemy that Holland could fear was Germany, but an invasion from that quarter could be easily repulsed by cutting the dikes and drowning the invaders. The sea, he taught Boyne, was the great defence of Holland, and it was a waste of money to keep such an army as the Dutch had; but neither the sea nor the sword could drive out the Germans if once they insidiously married a Prussian prince to the Dutch Queen.

There seemed to be no getting away from the Queen, for Boyne. The valet not only talked about her, as the pleasantest subject which he could find, but he insisted upon showing Boyne all her palaces. He took him into the Parliament house, and showed him where she sat while the queen-mother read the address from the throne. He introduced him at a bazar where the shop-girl who spoke English better than Boyne, or at least without the central Ohio accent, wanted to sell him a miniature of the Queen on porcelain. She said the Queen was such a nice girl, and she was herself such a nice girl that Boyne blushed a little in looking at her. He bought the miniature, and then he did not know what to do with it; if any of the family, if Lottie, found out that he had it, or that Trannel, he should have no peace any more. He put it in his pocket, provisionally, and when he came giddily out of the shop he felt himself taken by the elbow and placed against the wall by the valet, who said the queens were coming. They drove down slowly through the crowded, narrow street, bowing right and left to the people flattened against the shops, and again Boyne saw her so near that he could have reached out his hand and almost touched hers.

The consciousness of this was so strong in him that he wondered whether he had not tried to do so. If he had he would have been arrested - he knew that; and so he knew that he had not done it. He knew that he imagined doing so because it would be so awful to have done it, and he imagined being in love with her because it would be so frantic. At the same time he dramatized an event in which he died for her, and she became aware of his hopeless passion at the last moment, while the anarchist from whom he had saved her confessed that the bomb had been meant for her. Perhaps it was a pistol.

He escaped from the valet as soon as he could, and went back to Scheveningen limp from this experience, but the queens were before him. They had driven down to visit the studio of a famous Dutch painter there, and again the doom was on Boyne to press forward with the other spectators and wait for the queens to appear and get into their carriage. The young Queen's looks were stamped in Boyne's consciousness, so that he saw her wherever he turned, like the sun when one has gazed at it. He thought how that Trannel had said he ought to hand her into her carriage, and he shrank away for fear he should try to do so, but he could not leave the place till she had come out with the queen - mother and driven off. Then he went slowly and breathlessly into the hotel, feeling the Queen's miniature in his pocket. It made his heart stand still, and then bound forward. He wondered again what he should do with it. If he kept it, Lottie would be sure to find it, and he could not bring himself to the sacrilege of destroying it. He thought he would walk out on the breakwater as far as he could and throw it into the sea, but when he got to the end of the mole he could not do so. He decided that he would give it to Ellen to keep for him, and not let Lottie see it; or perhaps he might pretend he had bought it for her. He could not do that, though, for it would not be true, and if he did he could not ask her to keep it from Lottie.

At dinner Mr. Trannel told him he ought to have been there to see the Queen; that she had asked especially for him, and wanted to know if they had not sent up her card to him. Boyne meditated an apt answer through all the courses, but he had not thought of one when they had come to the 'corbeille de fruits', and he was forced to go to bed without having avenged himself.

In taking rooms for her family at the hotel, Lottie had arranged for her emancipation from the thraldom of rooming with Ellen. She said that had gone on long enough; if she was grown up at all, she was grown up enough to have a room of her own, and her mother had yielded to reasoning which began and ended with this position. She would have interfered so far as to put Lottie into the room next her, but Lottie said that if Boyne was the baby he ought to be next his mother; Ellen might come next him, but she was going to have the room that was furthest from any implication of the dependence in which she had languished; and her mother submitted again. Boyne was not sorry; there had always been hours of the night when he felt the need of getting at his mother for reassurance as to forebodings which his fancy conjured up to trouble him in the wakeful dark. It was understood that he might freely do this, and though the judge inwardly fretted, he could not deny the boy the comfort of his mother's encouraging love. Boyne's visits woke him, but he slept the better for indulging in the young nerves that tremor from impressions against which the old nerves are proof. But now, in the strange fatality which seemed to involve him, Boyne could not go to his mother. It was too weirdly intimate, even for her; besides, when he had already tried to seek her counsel she had ignorantly repelled him.

The night after his day in The Hague, when he could bear it no longer, he put on his dressing-gown and softly opened Ellen's door, "awake, Ellen?" he whispered.

"Yes, What is it, Boyne" her gentle voice asked.

"He came and sat down by her bed and stole his hand into hers, which she put out to him. The watery moonlight dripped into the room at the edges of the shades, and the long wash of the sea made itself regularly heard on the sands.

"Can't you sleep?" Ellen asked again. "Are you homesick?"

"Not exactly that. But it does seem rather strange for us to be off here so far, doesn't it?"

"Yes, I don't see how I can forgive myself for making you come," said Ellen, but her voice did not sound as if she were very unhappy.

"You couldn't help it," said Boyne, and the words suggested a question to him. "Do you believe that such things are ordered, Ellen?"

"Everything is ordered, isn't it?"

"I suppose so. And if they are, we're not, to blame for what happens."

"Not if we try to do right."

"Of course. The Kentons always do that," said Boyne, with the faith in his family that did not fail him in the darkest hour. "But what I mean is that if anything comes on you that you can't foresee and you can't get out of -" The next step was not clear, and Boyne paused. He asked,

"Do you think that we can control our feelings, Ellen?"

"About what?"

"Well, about persons that we like." He added, for safety, "Or dislike."

"I'm afraid not," said Ellen, sadly, "We ought to like persons and dislike them for some good reason, but we don't."

"Yes, that's what I mean," said Borne, with a long breath. "Sometimes it seems like a kind of possession, doesn't it?"

"It seems more like that when we like them," Ellen said.

"Yes, that's what I mean. If a person was to take a fancy to some one that was above him, that was richer, or older, he wouldn't be to blame for it, would he?"

"Was that what you wanted to ask me about?"

Borne hesitated. "Yes" he said. He was in for it now.

Ellen had not noticed Boyne's absorption with Miss Rasmith on the ship, but she vaguely remembered hearing Lottie tease him about her, and she said now, "He wouldn't be to blame for it if he couldn't help it, but if the person was much older it would be a pity!"

"Uh, she isn't so very much older," said Borne, more cheerfully than he had spoken before.

"Is it somebody that you have taken a fancy to Borne?"

"I don't know, Ellen. That's what makes it so kind of awful. I can't tell whether it's a real fancy, or I only think it is. Sometimes I think it is, and sometimes I think that I think so because I am afraid to believe it. Do you under Ellen?"

"It seems to me that I do. But you oughtn't to let your fancy run away with you, Boyne. What a queer boy!"

"It's a kind of fascination, I suppose. But whether it's a real fancy or an unreal one, I can't get away from it."

"Poor boy!" said his sister.

"Perhaps it's those books. Sometimes I think it is, and I laugh at the whole idea; and then again it's so strong that I can't get away from it. Ellen!"

"Well, Boyne?"

"I could tell you who it is, if you think that would do any good - if you think it would help me to see it in the true light, or you could help me more by knowing who it is than you can now."

"I hope it isn't anybody that you can't respect, Boyne?"

"No, indeed! It's somebody you would never dream of."

"Well?" Ellen was waiting for him to speak, but he could not get the words out, even to her.

"I guess I'll tell you some other time. Maybe I can get over it myself."

"It would be the best way if you could."

He rose and left her bedside, and then he came back. "Ellen, I've got something that I wish you would keep for me."

"What is it? Of course I will."

"Well, it's - something I don't want you to let Lottie know I've got. She tells that Mr. Trannel everything, and then he wants to make fun. Do you think he's so very witty?"

"I can't help laughing at some things he says."

"I suppose he is," Boyne ruefully admitted. "But that doesn't make you like him any better. Well, if you won't tell Lottie, I'll give it to you now."

"I won't tell anything that you don't want me to, Boyne."

"It's nothing. It's just-a picture of the Queen on porcelain, that I got in The Hague. The guide took me into the store, and I thought I ought to get something."

"Oh, that's very nice, Boyne. I do like the Queen so much. She's so sweet!"

"Yes, isn't she?" said Boyne, glad of Ellen's approval. So far, at least, he was not wrong. "Here it is now."

He put the miniature in Ellen's hand. She lifted herself on her elbow. "Light the candle and let me see it."

"No, no!" he entreated. "It might wake Lottie, and - and - Good-night, Ellen."

"Can you go to sleep now, Boyne?"

"Oh yes. I'm all right. Good-night."

"Good-night, then."

Borne stooped over and kissed her, and went to the door. He came back and asked, "You don't think it was silly, or anything, for me to get it?"

"No, indeed! It's just what you will like to have when you get home. We've all seen her so often. I'll put it in my trunk, and nobody shall know about it till we're safely back in Tuskingum."

Boyne sighed deeply. "Yes, that's what I meant. Good-night."

"Good-night, Boyne."

"I hope I haven't waked you up too much?"

"Oh no. I can get to sleep easily again."

"Well, good-night." Boyne sighed again, but not so deeply, and this time he went out.

William Dean Howells

XXII

Mrs. Kenton woke with the clear vision which is sometimes vouchsafed to people whose eyes are holden at other hours of the day. She had heard Boyne opening and shutting Ellen's door, and her heart smote her that he should have gone to his sister with whatever trouble he was in rather than come to his mother. It was natural that she should put the blame on her husband, and "Now, Mr. Kenton," she began, with an austerity of voice which he recognized before he was well awake, "if you won't take Boyne off somewhere to-day, I will. I think we had better all go. We have been here a whole fortnight, and we have got thoroughly rested, and there is no excuse for our wasting our time any longer. If we are going to see Holland, we had better begin doing it."

The judge gave a general assent, and said that if she wanted to go to Flushing he supposed he could find some garden-seeds there, in the flower and vegetable nurseries, which would be adapted to the climate of Tuskingum, and they could all put in the day pleasantly, looking round the place. Whether it was the suggestion of Tuskingum in relation to Flushing that decided her against the place, or whether she had really meant to go to Leyden, she now expressed the wish, as vividly as if it were novel, to explore the scene of the Pilgrims' sojourn before they sailed for Plymouth, and she reproached him for not caring about the place when they both used to take such an interest in it at home.

"Well," said the judge, "if I were at home I should take an

interest in it here."

This provoked her to a silence which he thought it best to break in tacit compliance with her wish, and he asked, "Do you propose taking the whole family and the appurtenances? We shall be rather a large party."

"Ellen would wish to go, and I suppose Mr. Breckon. We couldn't very well go without them."

"And how about Lottie and that young Trannel?"

"We can't leave him out, very well. I wish we could. I don't like him."

"There's nothing easier than not asking him, if you don't want him."

"Yes, there is, when you've got a girl like Lottie to deal with. Quite likely she would ask him herself. We must take him because we can't leave her."

"Yes, I reckon," the judge acquiesced.

"I'm glad," Mrs. Kenton said, after a moment, "that it isn't Ellen he's after; it almost reconciles me to his being with Lottie so much. I only wonder he doesn't take to Ellen, he's so much like that -"

She did not say out what was in her mind, but her husband knew. "Yes, I've noticed it. This young Breckon was quite enough so, for my taste. I don't know what it is that just saves him from it."

"He's good. You could tell that from the beginning."

They went off upon the situation that, superficially or subliminally, was always interesting them beyond anything in the world, and they did not openly recur to Mrs. Kenton's

William Dean Howells

plan for the day till they met their children at breakfast. It was a meal at which Breckon and Trammel were both apt to join them, where they took it at two of the tables on the broad, seaward piazza of the hotel when the weather was fine. Both the young men now applauded her plan, in their different sorts. It was easily arranged that they should go by train and not by tram from The Hague. The train was chosen, and Mrs. Kenton, when she went to her room to begin the preparations for a day's pleasure which constitute so distinctly a part of its pain, imagined that everything was settled. She had scarcely closed the door behind her when Lottie opened it and shut it again behind her.

"Mother," she said, in the new style of address to which she was habituating Mrs. Kenton, after having so long called her momma, "I am not going with you."

"Indeed you are, then!" her mother retorted. "Do you think I would leave you here all day with that fellow? A nice talk we should make!"

"You are perfectly welcome to that fellow, mother, and as he's accepted he will have to go with you, and there won't be any talk. But, as I remarked before, I am not going."

"Why aren't you going, I should like to know?"

"Because I don't like the company."

"What do you mean? Have you got anything against Mr. Breckon?"

"He's insipid, but as long as Ellen don't mind it I don't care. I object to Mr. Trannel!"

"Why?"

"I don't see why I should have to tell you. If I said I liked him you might want to know, but it seems to me that my not liking him is - my not liking him is my own affair." There was a kind of logic in this that silenced Mrs. Kenton for the moment. In view of her advantage Lottie relented so far as to add, "I've found out something about him."

Mrs. Kenton was imperative in her alarm. "What is it?" she demanded.

Lottie answered, obliquely: "Well, I didn't leave The Hague to get rid of them, and then take up with one of them at Scheveningen."

"One of what?"

"COOK'S TOURISTS, if you must know, mother. Mr. Trannel, as you call him, is a Cook's tourist, and that's the end of it. I have got no use for him from this out."

Mrs. Kenton was daunted, and not for the first time, by her daughter's superior knowledge of life. She could put Boyne down sometimes, though not always, when he attempted to impose a novel code of manners or morals upon her, but she could not cope with Lottie. In the present case she could only ask, "Well?"

"Well, they're the cheapest of the cheap. He actually showed me his coupons, and tried to put me down with the idea that everybody used them. But I guess he found it wouldn't work. He said if you were not personally conducted it was all right."

"Now, Lottie, you have got to tell me just what you mean," said Mrs. Kenton, and from having stood during this parley, she sat down to hear Lottie out at her leisure. But if there was anything more difficult than for Lottie to be explicit it was to make her be so, and in the end Mrs. Kenton was scarcely wiser than she was at the beginning to her daughter's reasons. It appeared that if you wanted to be cheap you could travel with those coupons, and Lottie did not wish to be cheap, or have anything to do with those who were. The Kentons had always held up their heads, and if Ellen had chosen to disgrace them with Bittridge, Dick had made it all right, and she at least was not going to do anything that she would be ashamed of. She was going to stay at home, and have her meals in her room till they got back.

Her mother paid no heed to her repeated declaration. "Lottie," she asked, with the heart-quake that the thought of Richard's act always gave her with reference to Ellen, "have you ever let out the least hint of that?"

"Of course I haven't," Lottie scornfully retorted. "I hope I know what a crank Ellen is."

They were not just the terms in which Mrs. Kenton would have chosen to be reassured, but she was glad to be assured in any terms. She said, vaguely: "I believe in my heart that I will stay at home, too. All this has given me a bad headache."

"I was going to have a headache myself," said Lottie, with injury. "But I suppose I can get on along without. I can just simply say I'm not going. If he proposes to stay, too, I can soon settle that."

"The great difficulty will be to get your father to go."

"You can make Ellen make him," Lottie suggested.

"That is true," said Mrs. Kenton, with such increasing absence that her daughter required of her:

"Are you staying on my account?"

"I think you had better not be left alone the whole day. But I am not staying on your account. I don't believe we had so many of us better go. It might look a little pointed."

Lottie laughed harshly. "I guess Mr. Breckon wouldn't see the point, he's so perfectly gone."

"Do you really believe it, Lottie?" Mrs. Kenton entreated, with a sudden tenderness for her younger daughter such as she did not always feel.

"I should think anybody would believe it - anybody but Ellen."

"Yes," Mrs. Kenton dreamily assented.

Lottie made her way to the door. "Well, if you do stay, mother, I'm not going to have you hanging round me all day. I can chaperon myself."

"Lottie," her mother tried to stay her, "I wish you would go. I don't believe that Mr. Trannel will be much of an addition. He will be on your poor father's hands all day, or else Ellen's, and if you went you could help off."

"Thank you, mother. I've had quite all I want of Mr. Trannel. You can tell him he needn't go, if you want to."

Lottie at least did not leave her mother to make her excuses to the party when they met for starting. Mrs. Kenton had deferred her own till she thought it was too late for her husband to retreat, and then bunglingly made them, with so much iteration that it seemed to her it would have been far less pointed, as concerned Mr. Breckon, if she had gone. Lottie sunnily announced that she was going to stay with her mother, and did not even try to account for her defection to Mr. Trannel.

"What's the matter with my staying, too?" he asked. "It seems to me there are four wheels to this coach now."

He had addressed his misgiving more to Lottie than the rest; but with the same sunny indifference to the consequence for others that she had put on in stating her decision, she now discharged herself from further responsibility by turning on her heel and leaving it with the party generally. In the circumstances Mr. Trannel had no choice but to go, and he was supported, possibly, by the hope of taking it out of Lottie some other time.

It was more difficult for Mrs. Kenton to get rid of the judge, but an inscrutable frown goes far in such exigencies. It seems to explain, and it certainly warns, and the husband on whom it is bent never knows, even after the longest experience, whether he had better inquire further. Usually he decides that he had better not, and Judge Kenton went off towards the tram with Boyne in the cloud of mystery which involved them both as to Mrs. Kenton's meaning.

XXIII

Trannel attached himself as well as he could to Breckon and Ellen, and Breckon had an opportunity not fully offered him before to note a likeness between himself and a fellow-man whom he was aware of not liking, though he tried to love him, as he felt it right to love all men. He thought he had not been quite sympathetic enough with Mrs. Kenton in her having to stay behind, and he tried to make it up to Mr. Trannel in his having to come. He invented civilities to show him, and ceded his place next Ellen as if Trannel had a right to it. Trannel ignored him in keeping it, unless it was recognizing Breckon to say, "Oh, I hope I'm not in your way, old fellow?" and then making jokes to Ellen. Breckon could not say the jokes were bad, though the taste of them seemed to him so. The man had a fleeting wit, which scorched whatever he turned it upon, and yet it was wit. "Why don't you try him in American?" he asked at the failure of Breckon and the tram conductor to understand each other in Dutch. He tried the conductor himself in American, and he was so deplorably funny that it was hard for Breckon to help being 'particeps criminus', at least in a laugh.

He asked himself if that were really the kind of man he was, and he grew silent and melancholy in the fear that it was a good deal the sort of man. To this morbid fancy Trannel seemed himself in a sort of excess, or what he would be if he were logically ultimated. He remembered all the triviality of his behavior with Ellen at first, and rather sickened at the thought of some of his early pleasantries. She was talking gayly now with Trannel, and Breckon wondered whether she was falling under the charm that he felt in him, in spite of himself.

If she was, her father was not. The judge sat on the other side of the car, and unmistakably glowered at the fellow's attempts to make himself amusing to Ellen. Trannel himself was not insensible to the judge's mood. Now and then he said something to intensify it. He patronized the judge and he made fun of the tourist character in which Boyne had got himself up, with a field-glass slung by a strap under one arm and a red Baedeker in his hand. He sputtered with malign laughter at a rather gorgeous necktie which Boyne had put on for the day, and said it was not a very good match for the Baedeker.

Boyne retorted rudely, and that amused Trannel still more. He became personal to Breckon, and noted the unclerical cut of his clothes. He said he ought to have put on his uniform for an expedition like that, in case they got into any sort of trouble. To Ellen alone he was inoffensive, unless he overdid his polite attentions to her in carrying her parasol for her, and helping her out of the tram, when they arrived, shouldering every one else away, and making haste to separate her from the others and then to walk on with her a little in advance.

Suddenly he dropped her, and fell back to Boyne and his father, while Breckon hastened forward to her side. Trannel put his arm across Boyne's shoulders and asked him if he were mad, and then laughed at him. "You're all right, Boyne, but you oughtn't to be so approachable. You ought to put on more dignity, and repel familiarity!"

Boyne could only twitch away in silence that he made as haughty as he could, but not so haughty that Trannel did not find it laughable, and he laughed in a teasing way that made Breckon more and more serious. He was aware of becoming even solemn with the question of his likeness to Trannel. He was of Trannel's quality, and their difference was a matter of quantity, and there was not enough difference. In his sense of their likeness Breckon vowed himself to a gravity of behavior evermore which he should not probably be able to observe, but the sample he now displayed did not escape the keen vigilance of Trannel.

"With the exception of Miss Kenton," he addressed himself to the party, "you're all so easy and careless that if you don't look out you'll lose me. Miss Kenton, I wish you would keep an eye on me. I don't want to get lost."

Ellen laughed - she could not help it - and her laughing made it less possible than before for Breckon to unbend and meet Trannel on his own ground, to give him joke for joke, to exchange banter with him. He might never have been willing to do that, but now he shrank from it, in his realization of their likeness, with an abhorrence that rendered him rigid.

The judge was walking ahead with Boyne, and his back expressed such severe disapproval that, between her fear that Trannel would say something to bring her father's condemnation on him and her sense of their inhospitable attitude towards one who was their guest, in a sort, she said, with her gentle gayety, "Then you must keep near me, Mr. Trannel. I'll see that nothing happens."

"That's very sweet of you," said Trannel, soberly. Whether he had now vented his malicious humor and was ready to make himself agreeable, or was somewhat quelled by the unfriendly ambient he had created, or was wrought upon by her friendliness, he became everything that could be wished in a companion for a day's pleasure. He took the lead at thestation, and got them a compartment in the car to themselves for the little run to Leyden, and on the way he talked very well. He politely borrowed Boyne's Baedeker, and decided for the party what they had best see, and showed an acceptable intelligence, as well as a large experience in the claims of Leyden upon the visitor's interest. He had been there often before, it seemed, and in the event it appeared that he had chosen the days sightseeing wisely.

He no longer addressed himself respectfully to Ellen alone, but he re-established himself in Boyne's confidence with especial pains, and he conciliated Breckon by a recognition of his priority with Ellen with a delicacy refined enough for even the susceptibility of a lover alarmed for his rights. If he could not overcome the reluctance of the judge, he brought him to the civil response which any one who tried for Kenton's liking achieved, even if he did not merit it, and there remained no more reserve in Kenton's manner than there had been with the young man from the first. He had never been a persona grata to the judge, and if he did not become so now, he at least ceased to be actively displeasing.

That was the year before the young Queen came to her own, and in the last days of her minority she was visiting all the cities of her future dominion with the queen-mother. When Kenton's party left the station they found Leyden as gay for her reception as flags and banners could make the gray old town, and Trannel relapsed for a moment so far as to suggest that the decorations were in honor of Boyne's presence, but he did not abuse the laugh that this made to Boyne's further shame.

There was no carriage at the station which would hold the party of five, and they had to take two vehicles. Trannel said it was lucky they wanted two, since there were no more, and he put himself in authority to assort the party. The judge, he decided, must go with Ellen and Breckon, and he hoped Boyne would let him go in his carriage, if he would sit on the box with the driver. The judge afterwards owned that he had weakly indulged his dislike of the fellow, in letting him take Boyne, and not insisting on going himself with Tramiel, but this was when it was long too late. Ellen had her misgivings, but, except for that gibe about the decorations, Trannel had been behaving so well that she hoped she might trust Boyne with him. She made a kind of appeal for her brother, bidding him and Trannel take good care of each other, and Trannel promised so earnestly to look after Boyne that she ought to have been alarmed for him. He took the lead, rising at times to wave a reassuring hand to her over the back of his carriage, and, in fact, nothing evil could very well happen from him, with the others following so close upon him. They met from time to time in the churches they visited, and when they lost sight of one another, through a difference of opinion in the drivers as to the best route, they came together at the place Trannel had appointed for their next reunion.

He showed himself a guide so admirably qualified that he found a way for them to objects of interest that had at first denied themselves in anticipation of the visit from the queens; when they all sat down at lunch in the restaurant which he found for them, he could justifiably boast that he would get them into the Town Hall, which they had been told was barred for the day against anything but sovereign curiosity. He was now on the best term with Boyne, who seemed to have lost all diffidence of him, and treated him with an easy familiarity that showed itself in his slapping him on the shoulder and making dints in his hat. Trannel seemed to enjoy these caresses, and, when they parted again for the afternoon's sight-seeing, Ellen had no longer a qualm in letting Boyne drive off with him.

He had, in fact, known how to make himself very acceptable to Boyne. He knew all the originals of his heroical romances, and was able to give the real names and the geographical position of those princesses who had been in love with American adventurers. Under promise of secrecy he disclosed the real names of the adventurers themselves, now obscured in the titles given them to render them worthy their union with sovereigns. He resumed his fascinating confidences when they drove off after luncheon, and he resumed them after each separation from the rest of the party. Boyne listened with a flushed face and starting eyes, and when at last Trannel offered, upon a pledge of the most sacred nature from him never to reveal a word of what he said, he began to relate an adventure of which he was himself the hero. It was a bold travesty of one of the latest romances that Boyne had read, involving the experience of an American very little older than

Boyne himself, to whom a wilful young crown-princess, in a little state which Trannel would not name even to Boyne, had made advances such as he could not refuse to meet without cruelty. He was himself deeply in love with her, but he felt bound in honor not to encourage her infatuation as long as he could help, for he had been received by her whole family with such kindness and confidence that he had to consider them.

"Oh, pshaw!" Boyne broke in upon him, doubting, and yet wishing not to doubt, "that's the same as the story of 'Hector Folleyne'."

"Yes," said Trannel, quietly. "I thought you would recognize it."

"Well, but," Boyne went on, "Hector married the princess!"

"In the book, yes. The fellow I gave the story to said it would never do not to have him marry her, and it would help to disguise the fact. That's what he said, after he had given the whole thing away."

"And do you mean to say it was you? Oh, you can't stuff me! How did you get out of marrying her, I should like to know, when the chancellor came to you and said that the whole family wanted you to, for fear it would kill her if -"

"Well, there was a scene, I can't deny that. We had a regular family conclave - father, mother, Aunt Hitty, and all the folks - and we kept it up pretty much all night. The princess wasn't there, of course, and I could convince them that I was right. If she had been, I don't believe I could have held out. But they had to listen to reason, and I got away between two days."

"But why didn't you marry her?"

"Well, for one thing, as I told you, I thought I ought to consider her family. Then there was a good fellow, the crown-prince of Saxe-Wolfenhutten, who was dead in love with her, and was engaged to her before I turned up. I had been at school with him, and I felt awfully sorry for him; and I thought I ought to sacrifice myself a little to him. But I suppose the thing that influenced me most was finding out that if I married the princess I should have to give up my American citizenship and become her subject."

"Well?" Boyne panted.

"Well, would you have done it?"

"Couldn't you have got along without doing that?"

"That was the only thing I couldn't get around, somehow. So I left."

"And the princess, did she - die?"

"It takes a good deal more than that to kill a fifteen-year-old princess," said Trannel, and he gave a harsh laugh. "She married Saxe-Wolfenhutten." Boyne was silent. "Now, I don't want you to speak of this till after I leave Scheveningen - especially to Miss Lottie. You know how girls are, and I think Miss Lottie is waiting to get a bind on me, anyway. If she heard how I was cut out of my chance with that princess she'd never let me believe I gave her up of my own free will?"

"NO, no; I won't tell her."

Boyne remained in a silent rapture, and he did not notice they were no longer following the rest of their party in the other carriage. This had turned down a corner, at which Mr. Breckon, sitting on the front seat, had risen and beckoned their driver to follow, but their driver, who appeared afterwards to have not too much a head of his own, or no head at all, had continued straight on, in the rear of a tram-car, which was slowly finding its way through the momently thickening crowd. Boyne was first aware that it was a humorous crowd when, at a turn of the street, their equipage was greeted with ironical cheers by a group of gay young Dutchmen on the sidewalk. Then he saw that the sidewalks were packed with people, who spread into the street almost to the tram, and that the house fronts were dotted with smiling Dutch faces, the faces of pretty Dutch girls, who seemed to share the amusement of the young fellows below.

Trannel lay back in the carriage. "This is something like," he said. "Boyne, they're on to the distinguished young Ohioan - the only Ohioan out of office in Europe."

"Yes," said Boyne, trying to enjoy it. "I wonder what they are holloing at."

Trannel laughed. "They're holloing at your Baedeker, my dear boy. They never saw one before," and Boyne was aware that he was holding his red-backed guide conspicuously in view on his lap. "They know you're a foreigner by it."

"Don't you think we ought to turn down somewhere? I don't see poppa anywhere." He rose and looked anxiously back over the top of their carriage. The crowd, closing in behind it, hailed his troubled face with cries that were taken up by the throng on the sidewalks. Boyne turned about to find that the tram-car which they had been following had disappeared round a corner, but their driver was still keeping on. At a wilder burst of applause Trannel took off his hat and bowed to the crowd, right and left.

"Bow, bow!" he said to Boyne. "They'll be calling for a speech the next thing. Bow, I tell you!"

"Tell him to turn round!" cried the boy.

"I can't speak Dutch," said Trannel, and Boyne leaned forward and poked the driver in the back.

"Go back!" he commanded.

The driver shook his head and pointed forward with his whip. "He's all right," said Trannel. "He can't turn now. We've got to take the next corner." The street in front was empty, and the people were crowding back on the sidewalks. Loud, vague noises made themselves heard round the corner to which the driver had pointed. "By Jove!" Trannel said, "I believe they're coming round that way."

"Who are coming?" Boyne palpitated.

"The queens."

"The queens?" Boyne gasped; it seemed to him that he shrieked the words.

"Yes. And there's a tobacconist's now," said Trannel, as if that were what he had been looking for all along. "I want some cigarettes."

He leaped lightly from the carriage, and pushed his way out of sight on the sidewalk. Boyne remained alone in the vehicle, staring wildly round; the driver kept slowly and stupidly on, Boyne did not know how much farther. He could not speak; he felt as if he could not stir. But the moment came when he could not be still. He gave a galvanic jump to the ground, and the friendly crowd on the sidewalk welcomed him to its ranks and closed about him. The driver had taken the lefthand corner, just before a plain carriage with the Queen and the queen-mother came in sight round the right. The young Queen was bowing to the people, gently, and with a sort of mechanical regularity. Now and then a brighter smile than that she conventionally wore lighted up her face. The simple progress was absolutely without state, except for the aide-de-camp on horseback who rode beside the carriage, a little to the front.

Boyne stood motionless on the curb, where a friendly tall Dutchman had placed him in front that he might see the Queen.

"Hello!" said the voice of Trannel, and elbowing his way to Boyne's side, he laughed and coughed through the smoke of his cigarette. "I was afraid you had lost me. Where's your carriage?"

Boyne did not notice his mockeries. He was entranced in that beatific vision; his boy-heart went out in worship to the pretty young creature with a reverence that could not be uttered. The tears came into his eyes.

"There, there! She's bowing to you, Boyne, she's smiling right at you. By Jove! She's beckoning to you!"

"You be still!" Boyne retorted, finding his tongue. "She isn't doing any such a thing."

"She is, I swear she is! She's doing it again! She's stopping the carriage. Oh, go out and see what she wants! Don't you know that a queen's wish is a command? You've got to go!"

Boyne never could tell just how it happened. The carriage did seem to be stopping, and the Queen seemed to be looking at him. He thought he must, and he started into the street towards her, and the carriage came abreast of him. He had almost reached the carriage when the aide turned and spurred his horse before him. Four strong hands that were like iron clamps were laid one on each of Boyne's elbows and shoulders, and he was haled away, as if by superhuman force. "Mr. Trannel!" he called out. in his agony, but the wretch had disappeared, and Boyne was left with his captors, to whom he could have said nothing if he could have thought of anything to say.

The detectives pulled him through the crowd and hurried him swiftly down the side street. A little curiosity straggled after him in the shape of small Dutch boys, too short to look over the shoulders of men at the queens, and too weak to make their way through them to the front; but for them, Boyne seemed alone in the world with the relentless officers, who were dragging him forward and hurting him so with the grip of their iron hands. He lifted up his face to entreat them not to hold him so tight, and suddenly it was as if he beheld an angel standing in his path. It was Breckon who was there, staring at him aghast.

"Why, Boyne!" he cried.

"Oh, Mr. Breckon!" Boyne wailed back. "Is it you? Oh, do tell them I didn't mean to do anything! I thought she beckoned to me."

"Who? Who beckoned to you?"

"The Queen!" Boyne sobbed, while the detectives pulled him relentlessly on.

Breckon addressed them suavely in their owe tongue which had never come in more deferential politeness from human lips. He ventured the belief that there was a mistake; he assured them that he knew their prisoner, and that he was the son of a most respectable American family, whom they could find at the Kurhaus in Scheveningen. He added some irrelevancies, and got for all answer that they had made Boyne's arrest for sufficient reasons, and were taking him to prison. If his friends wished to intervene in his behalf they could do so before the magistrate, but for the present they must admonish Mr. Breckon not to put himself in the way of the law.

"Don't go, Mr. Breckon!" Boyne implored him, as his captors made him quicken his pace after slowing a little for their colloquy with Breckon. "Oh, where is poppa? He could get me away. Oh, where is poppa?"

"Don't! Don't call out, Boyne," Breckon entreated. "Your father is right here at the end of the street. He's in the carriage there with Miss Kenton. I was coming to look for you. Don't cry out so!"

"No, no, I won't, Mr. Breckon. I'll be perfectly quiet now. Only do get poppa quick! He can tell them in a minute that it's all right!"

He made a prodigious effort to control himself, while Breckon ran a little ahead, with some wild notion of preparing Ellen. As he disappeared at the corner, Boyne choked a sob into a muffed bellow, and was able to meet the astonished eyes of his father and sister in this degree of triumph.

They had not in the least understood Breckon's explanation, and, in fact, it had not been very lucid. At sight of her brother strenuously upheld between the detectives, and dragged along the sidewalk, Ellen sprang from the carriage and ran towards him. "Why, what's the matter with Boyne?" she demanded. "Are you hurt, Boyne, dear? Are they taking him to the hospital?"

Before he could answer, and quite before the judge could reach the tragical group, she had flung her arms round Boyne's neck, and was kissing his tear-drabbled face, while he lamented back, "They're taking me to prison."

"Taking you to prison? I should like to know what for! What are you taking my brother to prison for?" she challenged the detectives, who paused, bewildered, while all the little Dutch boys round admired this obstruction of the law, and several Dutch housewives, too old to go out to see the queens, looked down from their windows. It was wholly illegal, but the detectives were human. They could snub such a friend of their prisoner as Breckon, but they could not meet the dovelike ferocity of Ellen with unkindness. They explained as well as they might, and at a suggestion which Kenton made through Breckon, they admitted that it was not beside their duty to take Boyne directly to a magistrate, who could pass upon his case, and even release him upon proper evidence of his harmlessness, and sufficient security for any demand that justice might make for his future appearance.

"Then," said the judge, quietly, "tell them that we will go with them. It will be all right, Boyne. Ellen, you and I will get back into the carriage, and -"

"No!" Boyne roared. "Don't leave me, Nelly!"

"Indeed, I won't leave you, Boyne! Mr. Breckon, you get into the carriage with poppa, and I -"

"I think I had better go with you, Miss Kenton," said Breckon, and in a tender superfluity they both accompanied Boyne on foot, while the judge remounted to his place in the carriage and kept abreast of them on their way to the magistrate's.

XXIV

The magistrate conceived of Boyne's case with a readiness that gave the judge a high opinion of his personal and national intelligence. He even smiled a little, in accepting the explanation which Breckon was able to make him from Boyne, but he thought his duty to give the boy a fatherly warning for the future. He remarked to Breckon that it was well for Boyne that the affair had not happened in Germany, where it would have been found a much more serious matter, though, indeed, he added, it had to be seriously regarded anywhere in these times, when the lives of sovereigns were so much at the mercy of all sorts of madmen and miscreants. He relaxed a little from his severity in his admonition to say directly to Boyne that queens, even when they wished to speak with people, did not beckon them in the public streets. When this speech translated to Boyne by Breckon, whom the magistrate complimented on the perfection of his Dutch, Boyne hung his head sheepishly, and could not be restored to his characteristic dignity again in the magistrate's presence. The judge gratefully shook hands with the friendly justice, and made him a little speech of thanks, which Breckon interpreted, and then the justice shook hand with the judge, and gracefully accepted the introduction which he offered him to Ellen. They parted with reciprocal praises and obeisances, which included even the detectives. The judge had some question, which he submitted to Breckon, whether he ought not to offer them something, but Breckon thought not.

Breckon found it hard to abdicate the sort of authority in

which his knowledge of Dutch had placed him, and when he protested that he had done nothing but act as interpreter, Ellen said, "Yes, but we couldn't have done anything without you," and this was the view that Mrs. Kenton took of the matter in the family conclave which took place later in the evening. Breckon was not allowed to withdraw from it, in spite of many modest efforts, before she had bashfully expressed her sense of his service to him, and made Boyne share her thanksgiving. She had her arm about the boy's shoulder in giving Breckon her hand, and when Breckon had got away she pulled Boyne to her in a more peremptory embrace.

"Now, Boyne," she said, "I am not going to have any more nonsense. I want to know why you did it."

The judge and Ellen had already conjectured clearly enough, and Boyne did not fear them. But he looked at his younger sister as he sulkily answered, "I am not going to tell you before Lottie."

"Come in here, then," said his mother, and she led him into the next room and closed the door. She quickly returned without him. "Yes," she began, "it's just as I supposed; it was that worthless fellow who put him up to it. Of course, it began with those fool books he's been reading, and the notions that Miss Rasmith put into his head. But he never would have done anything if it hadn't been for Mr. Trannel."

Lottie had listened in silent scorn to the whole proceedings up to this point, and had refused a part in the general recognition of Breckon as a special providence. Now she flashed out with a terrible volubility: "What did I tell you? What else could you expect of a Cook's tourist? And mom - mother wanted to make me go with you, after I told her what he was! Well, if I had have gone, I'll bet I could have kept him from playing his tricks. I'll bet he wouldn't have taken any liberties, with me along. I'll bet if he had, it wouldn't have been Boyne that got arrested. I'll bet he wouldn't have got off so easily with the magistrate, either! But I suppose you'll all let him come bowing and smiling round in the morning, like butter wouldn't melt in your mouths. That seems to be the Kenton way. Anybody can pull our noses, or get us arrested that wants to, and we never squeak." She went on a long time to this purpose, Mrs. Kenton listening with an air almost of conviction, and Ellen patiently bearing it as a right that Lottie had in a matter where she had been otherwise ignored.

The judge broke out, not upon Lottie, but upon his wife. "Good heavens, Sarah, can't you make the child hush?"

Lottie answered for her mother, with a crash of nerves and a gush of furious tears: "Oh, I've got to hush, I suppose. It's always the way when I'm trying to keep up the dignity of the family. I suppose it will be cabled to America, and by tomorrow it will be all over Tuskingum how Boyne was made a fool of and got arrested. But I bet there's one person in Tuskingum that won't have any remarks to make, and that's Bittridge. Not, as long as Dick's there he won't."

"Lottie!" cried her mother, and her father started towards her, while Ellen still sat patiently quiet.

"Oh, well!" Lottie submitted. "But if Dick was here I know this Trannel wouldn't get off so smoothly. Dick would give him a worse cowhiding than he did Bittridge."

Half the last word was lost in the bang of the door which Lottie slammed behind her, leaving her father and mother to a silence which Ellen did not offer to break. The judge had no heart to speak, in his dismay, and it was Mrs. Kenton who took the word.

"Ellen," she began, with compassionate gentleness, "we tried to keep it from you. We knew how you would feel. But now we have got to tell you. Dick did cowhide him when he got back to Tuskingum. Lottie wrote out to Dick about it, how Mr. Bittridge had behaved in New York. Your father and I didn't approve of it, and Dick didn't afterwards; but, yes, he did do it."

"I knew it, momma," said Ellen, sadly.

"You knew it! How?"

"That other letter I got when we first came - it was from his mother."

"Did she tell -"

"Yes. It was terrible she seemed to feel so. And I was sorry for her. I thought I ought to answer it, and I did. I told her I was sorry, too. I tried not to blame Richard. I don't believe I did. And I tried not to blame him. She was feeling badly enough without that."

Her father and mother looked at each other; they did not speak, and she asked, "Do you think I oughtn't to have written?"

Her father answered, a little tremulously: "You did right, Ellen. And I am sure that you did it in just the right way."

"I tried to. I thought I wouldn't worry you about it."

She rose, and now her mother thought she was going to say that it put an end to everything; that she must go back and offer herself as a sacrifice to the injured Bittridges. Her mind had reverted to that moment on the steamer when Ellen told her that nothing had reconciled her to what had happened with Bittridge but the fact that all the wrong done had been done to themselves; that this freed her. In her despair she could not forbear asking, "What did you write to her, Ellen?"

"Nothing. I just said that I was very sorry, and that I knew how she felt. I don't remember exactly."

She went up and kissed her mother. She seemed rather

fatigued than distressed, and her father asked her. "Are you going to bed, my dear?"

"Yes, I'm pretty tired, and I should think you would be, too, poppa. I'll speak to poor Boyne. Don't mind Lottie. I suppose she couldn't help saying it." She kissed her father, and slipped quietly into Boyne's room, from which they could hear her passing on to her own before they ventured to say anything to each other in the hopeful bewilderment to which she had left them.

"Well?" said the judge.

"Well?" Mrs. Kenton returned, in a note of exasperation, as if she were not going to let herself be forced to the initiative.

"I thought you thought -"

"I did think that. Now I don't know what to think. We have got to wait."

"I'm willing to wait for Ellen!"

"She seems," said Mrs. Kenton, "to have more sense than both the other children put together, and I was afraid -"

"She might easily have more sense than Boyne, or Lottie, either."

"Well, I don't know," Mrs. Kenton began. But she did not go on to resent the disparagement which she had invited. "What I was afraid of was her goodness. It was her goodness that got her into the trouble, to begin with. If she hadn't been so good, that fellow could never have fooled her as he did. She was too innocent."

The judge could not forbear the humorous view. "Perhaps she's getting wickeder, or not so innocent. At any rate, she doesn't seem to have been take in by Trannel."

"He didn't pay any attention to her. He was all taken up with Lottie."

"Well, that was lucky. Sarah," said the judge, "do you think he is like Bittridge?"

"He's made me think of him all the time."

"It's curious," the judge mused. "I have always noticed how our faults repeat themselves, but I didn't suppose our fates would always take the same shape, or something like it." Mrs. Kenton stared at him. "When this other one first made up to us on the boat my heart went down. I thought of Bittridge so."

"Mr. Breckon?"

"Yes, the same lightness; the same sort of trifling - Didn't you notice it?"

"No - yes, I noticed it. But I wasn't afraid for an instant. I saw that he was good."

"Oh!"

"What I'm afraid of now is that Ellen doesn't care anything about him."

"He isn't wicked enough?"

"I don't say that. But it would be too much happiness to expect in one short life."

The judge could not deny the reasonableness of her position. He could only oppose it. "Well, I don't think we've had any more than our share of happiness lately."

No one except Boyne could have made Trannel's behavior a cause of quarrel, but the other Kentons made it a cause of coldness which was quite as effective. In Lottie this took the form of something so active, so positive, that it was something more than a mere absence of warmth. Before she came clown to breakfast the next morning she studied a stare in her mirror, and practised it upon Trannel so successfully when he came up to speak to her that it must have made him doubt whether he had ever had her acquaintance. In his doubt he ventured to address her, and then Lottie turned her back upon him in a manner that was perfectly convincing. He attempted a smiling ease with Mrs. Kenton and the judge, but they shared neither his smile nor his ease, and his jocose questions about the end of yesterday's adventures, which he had not been privy to, did not seem to appeal to the American sense of humor in them. Ellen was not with them, nor Boyne, but Trannel was not asked to take either of the vacant places at the table, even when Breckon took one of them, after a decent exchange of civilities with him. He could only saunter away and leave Mrs. Kenton to a little pang.

"Tchk!" she made. "I'm sorry for him!"

"So am I," said the judge. "But he will get over it - only too soon, I'm afraid. I don't believe he's very sorry for himself."

They had not advised with Breckon, and he did not feel authorized to make any comment. He seemed preoccupied, to Mrs. Kenton's eye, when she turned it upon him from Trannel's discomfited back, lessening in the perspective, and he answered vaguely to her overture about his night's rest. Lottie never made any conversation with Breckon, and she now left him to himself, with some remnants of the disapproval which she found on her hands after crushing Trannel. It could not be said that Breckon was aware of her disapproval, and the judge had no apparent consciousness of it. He and Breckon tried to make something of each other, but failed, and it all seemed a very defeating sequel to Mrs. Kenton after the triumphal glow of the evening before. When Lottie rose, she went with her, alleging her wish to see if Boyne had eaten his breakfast. She confessed, to Breckon's kind inquiry, that Boyne did not seem very well, and that she had made him take his breakfast in his room, and she did not think it necessary to own, even to so friendly a witness as Mr. Breckon, that Boyne was ashamed to come down, and dreaded meeting Trannel so much that she was giving him time to recover his self-respect and courage.

As soon as she and Lottie were gone Breckon began, rather more formidably than he liked, but helplessly so: "Judge Kenton, I should be glad of a few moments with you on - on an important - on a matter that is important to me."

"Well," said the judge, cautiously. Whatever was coming, he wished to guard himself from the mistake that he had once so nearly fallen into, and that still made him catch his breath to think of. "How can I be of use to you?"

"I don't know that you can be of any use - I don't know that I ought to speak to you. But I thought you might perhaps save me from - save my taking a false step."

He looked at Kenton as if he would understand, and Kenton supposed that he did. He said, "My daughter once mentioned your wish to talk with me."

"Your daughter?" Breckon stared at him in stupefaction.

"Yes; Ellen. She said you wished to consult me about going back to your charge in New York, when we were on the ship together. But I don't know that I'm very competent to give advice in such -"

"Oh!" Breckon exclaimed, in a tone of immense relief, which did not continue itself in what he went on to say. "That! I've quite made up my mind to go back." He stopped, and then he burst out, "I want to speak with you about her." The judge sat steady, still resolute not to give himself away, and the young man scarcely recovered from what had been a desperate plunge in adding: "I know that it's usual to speak with her - with the lady herself first, but - I don't know! The circumstances are

William Dean Howells

peculiar. You only know about me what you've seen of me, and I would rather make my mistakes in the order that seems right to me, although it isn't just the American way."

He smiled rather piteously, and the judge said, rather encouragingly, "I don't quite know whether I follow you."

Breckon blushed, and sought help in what remained of his coffee. "The way isn't easy for me. But it's this: I ask your leave to ask Miss Ellen to marry me." The worst was over now, and looked as if it were a relief. "She is the most beautiful person in the world to me, and the best; but as you know so little of me, I thought it right to get your leave - to tell you - to - to - That is all." He fell back in his chair and looked a at Kenton.

"It is unusual," the judge began.

"Yes, Yes; I know that. And for that reason I speak first to you. I'll be ruled by you implicitly."

"I don't mean that," Kenton said. "I would have expected that you would speak to her first. But I get your point of view, and I must say I think you're right. I think you are behaving - honorably. I wish that every one was like you. But I can't say anything now. I must talk with her mother. My daughter's life has not been happy. I can't tell you. But as far as I am concerned, and I think Mrs. Kenton, too, I would be glad - We like you Mr. Breckon. We think you are a good man.

"Oh, thank you. I'm not so sure -"

"We'd risk it. But that isn't all. Will you excuse me if I don't say anything more just yet - and if I leave you?"

"Why, certainly." The judge had risen and pushed back his chair, and Breckon did the same. "And I shall - hear from you?"

"Why, certainly," said the judge in his turn.

"It isn't possible that you put him off!" his wife reproached him, when he told what had passed between him and Breckon. "Oh, you couldn't have let him think that we didn't want him for her! Surely you didn't!"

"Will you get it into your head," he flamed back, "that he hasn't spoken to Ellen yet, and I couldn't accept him till she had?"

"Oh yes. I forgot that." Mrs. Kenton struggled with the fact, in the difficulty of realizing so strange an order of procedure. "I suppose it's his being educated abroad that way. But, do go back to him, Rufus, and tell him that of course -"

"I will do nothing of the kind, Sarah! What are you thinking of?"

"Oh, I don't know what I'm thinking of! I must see Ellen, I suppose. I'll go to her now. Oh, dear, if she doesn't - if she lets such a chance slip through her fingers - But she's quite likely to, she's so obstinate! I wonder what she'll want us to do."

She fled to her daughter's room and found Boyne there, sitting beside his sister's bed, giving her a detailed account of his adventure of the day before, up to the moment Mr. Breckon met him, in charge of the detectives. Up to that moment, it appeared to Boyne, as nearly as he could recollect, that he had not broken down, but had behaved himself with a dignity which was now beginning to clothe his whole experience. In the retrospect, a quiet heroism characterized his conduct, and at the moment his mother entered the room he was questioning Ellen as to her impressions of his bearing when she first saw him in the grasp of the detectives.

His mother took him by the arm, and said, "I want to speak with Ellen, Boyne," and put him out of the door.

Then she came back and sat down in his chair. "Ellen. Mr. Breckon has been speaking to your father. Do you know what about?"

"About his going back to New York?" the girl suggested.

Her mother kept her patience with difficulty. "No, not about that. About you! He's asked your father - I can't understand yet why he did it, only he's so delicate and honorable, and goodness known we appreciate it - whether he can tell you that - that -" It was not possible for such a mother as Mrs. Kenton to say "He loves you"; it would have sounded as she would have said, too sickish, and she compromised on: "He likes you, and wants to ask you whether you will marry him. And, Ellen," she continued, in the ample silence which followed, "if you don't say you will, I will have nothing more to do With such a simpleton. I have always felt that you behaved very foolishly about Mr. Bittridge, but I hoped that when you grew older you would see it as we did, and - and behave differently. And now, if, after all we've been through with you, you are going to say that you won't have Mr. Breckon -"

Mrs. Kenton stopped for want of a figure that would convey all the disaster that would fall upon Ellen in such an event, and she was given further pause when the girl gently answered, "I'm not going to say that, momma."

"Then what in the world are you going to say?" Mrs. Kenton demanded.

Ellen had turned her face away on the pillow, and now she answered, quietly, "When Mr. Breckon asks me I will tell him."

"Well, you had better!" her mother threatened in return, and she did not realize the falsity of her position till she reported Ellen's words to the judge.

"Well, Sarah, I think she had you there," he said, and Mrs. Kenton then said that she did not care, if the child was only going to behave sensibly at last, and she did believe she was.

"Then it's all right" said the judge, and he took up the Tuskingum Intelligencer, lying till then unread in the excitements which had followed its arrival the day before, and began to read it.

Mrs. Kenton sat dreamily watching him, with her hands fallen in her lap. She suddenly started up, with the cry, "Good gracious! What are we all thinking of?"

Kenton stared at her over the top of his paper. "How, thinking of?"

"Why Mr. Breckon! He must be crazy to know what we've decided, poor fellow!"

"Oh," said the judge, folding the Intelligencer on his knee. "I had forgotten. Somehow, I thought it was all settled."

Mrs. Kenton took his paper from him, and finished folding it. "It hasn't begun to be settled. You must go and let him know."

"Won't he look me up?" the judge suggested.

"You must look him up. Go at once dear! Think how anxious he must be!"

Kenton was not sure that Breckon looked very anxious when he found him on the brick promenade before the Kurhaus, apparently absorbed in noting the convulsions of a large, round German lady in the water, who must have supposed herself to be bathing. But perhaps the young man did not see her; the smile on his face was too vague for such an interest when he turned at Kenton's approaching steps.

The judge hesitated for an instant, in which the smile left Breckon's face. "I believe that's all right, Mr. Breckon," he said. "You'll find Mrs. Kenton in our parlor," and then the

William Dean Howells

two men parted, with an "Oh, thank you!" from Breckon, who walked back towards the hotel, and left Kenton to ponder upon the German lady; as soon as he realized that she was not a barrel, the judge continued his walk along the promenade, feeling rather ashamed.

Mrs. Kenton had gone to Ellen's room again when she had got the judge off upon his mission. She rather flung in upon her. "Oh, you are up!" she apologized to Ellen's back. The girl's face was towards the glass, and she was tilting her head to get the effect of the hat on it, which she now took off.

"I suppose poppa's gone to tell him," she said, sitting tremulously down.

"Didn't you want him to?" her mother asked, stricken a little at sight of her agitation.

"Yes, I wanted him to, but that doesn't make it any easier. It makes it harder. Momma!"

"Well, Ellen?"

"You know you've got to tell him, first."

"Tell him?" Mrs. Kenton repeated, but she knew what Ellen meant.

"About - Mr. Bittridge. All about it. Every single thing. About his kissing me that night."

At the last demand Mrs. Kenton was visibly shaken in her invisible assent to the girl's wish. "Don't you think, Ellen, that you had better tell him that - some time?"

"No, now. And you must tell him. You let me go to the theatre with him." The faintest shadow of resentment clouded the girl's face, but still Mrs. Kenton, thought she knew her own guilt, could not yield.

"Why, Ellen," she pleaded, not without a reproachful sense of vulgarity in such a plea, "don't you suppose HE ever - kissed any one?"

"That doesn't concern me, momma," said Ellen, without a trace of consciousness that she was saying anything uncommon. "If you won't tell him, then that ends it. I won't see him."

"Oh, well!" her mother sighed. "I will try to tell him. But I'd rather be whipped. I know he'll laugh at me."

"He won't laugh at you," said the girl, confidently, almost comfortingly. "I want him to know everything before I meet him. I don't want to have a single thing on my mind. I don't want to think of myself!"

Mrs. Kenton understood the woman - soul that spoke in these words. "Well," she said, with a deep, long breath, "be ready, then."

But she felt the burden which had been put upon her to be so much more than she could bear that when she found her husband in their parlor she instantly resolved to cast it upon him. He stood at the window with his hat on.

"Has Breckon been here yet?" he asked.

"Have you seen him yet?" she returned.

"Yes, and I thought he was coming right here. But perhaps he stopped to screw his courage up. He only knew how little it needed with us!"

"Well, now, it's we who've got to have the courage. Or you have. Do you know what Ellen wants to have done?" Mrs. Kenton put it in these impersonal terms, and as a preliminary to shirking her share of the burden.

"She doesn't want to have him refused?"

"She wants to have him told all about Bittridge."

After a momentary revolt the judge said, "Well, that's right. It's like Ellen."

"There's something else that's more like her," said Mrs. Kenton, indignantly. "She wants him to told about what Bittridge did that night - about him kissing her."

The judge looked disgusted with his wife for the word; then he looked aghast. "About -"

"Yes, and she won't have a word to say to him till he is told, and unless he is told she will refuse him."

"Did she say that?"

"No, but I know she will."

"If she didn't say she would, I think we may take the chances that she won't."

"No, we mustn't take any such chances. You must tell him."

"I? No, I couldn't manage it. I have no tact, and it would sound so confoundedly queer, coming from one man to another. It would be - indelicate. It's something that nobody but a woman - Why doesn't she tell him herself?"

"She won't. She considers it our part, and something we ought to do before he commits himself."

"Very well, then, Sarah, you must tell him. You can manage it so it won't by so - queer.

"That is just what I supposed you would say, Mr. Kenton, but I must say I didn't expect it of you. I think it's cowardly."

"Look out, Sarah! I don't like that word."

"Oh, I suppose you're brave enough when it comes to any kind of danger. But when it comes to taking the brunt of anything unpleasant -"

"It isn't unpleasant - it's queer."

"Why do you keep saying that over and over? There's nothing queer about it. It's Ellenish but isn't it right?"

"It's right, yes, I suppose. But it's squeamish."

"I see nothing squeamish about it. But I know you're determined to leave it to me, and so I shall do it. I don't believe Mr. Breckon will think it's queer or squeamish."

"I've no doubt he'll take it in the right way; you'll know how to -" Kenton looked into his hat, which he had taken off and then put it on again. His tone and his manner were sufficiently sneaking, and he could not make them otherwise. It was for this reason, no doubt, that he would not prolong the interview.

"Oh yes, go!" said Mrs. Kenton, as he found himself with his hand on the door. "Leave it all to me, do!" and he was aware of skulking out of the room. By the time that it would have taken him so long as to walk to the top of the grand stairway he was back again. "He's coming!" he said, breathlessly. "I saw him at the bottom of the stairs. Go into your room and wash your eyes. I'LL tell him."

"No, no, Rufus! Let me! It will be much better. You'll be sure to bungle it."

"We must risk that. You were quite right, Sarah. It would have been cowardly in me to let you do it."

"Rufus! You know I didn't mean it! Surely you're not

resenting that?"

"No. I'm glad you made me see it. You're all right, Sarah, and you'll find that it will all come out all right. You needn't be afraid I'll bungle it. I shall use discretion. Go -"

"I shall not stir a step from this parlor! You've got back all your spirit, dear," said the old wife, with young pride in her husband. "But I must say that Ellen is putting more upon you than she has any right to. I think she might tell him herself."

"No, it's our business - my business. We allowed her to get in for it. She's quite right about it. We must not let him commit himself to her till he knows the thing that most puts her to shame. It isn't enough for us to say that it was really no shame. She feels that it casts a sort of stain - you know what I mean, Sarah, and I believe I can make this young man know. If I can't, so much the worse for him. He shall never see Ellen again."

"Oh, Rufus!"

"Do you think he would be worthy of her if he couldn't?"

"I think Ellen is perfectly ridiculous."

"Then that shows that I am right in deciding not to leave this thing to you. I feel as she does about it, and I intend that he shall."

"Do you intend to let her run the chance of losing him?"

"That is what I intend to do."

"Well, then, I'll tell you what: I am going to stay right here. We will both see him; it's right for us to do it." But at a rap on the parlor door Mrs. Kenton flew to that of her own room, which she closed upon her with a sort of Parthian whimper, "Oh, do be careful, Rufus!"

Whether Kenton was careful or not could never be known, from either Kenton himself or from Breckon. The judge did tell him everything, and the young man received the most damning details of Ellen's history with a radiant absence which testified that they fell upon a surface sense of Kenton, and did not penetrate to the all-pervading sense of Ellen herself below. At the end Kenton was afraid he had not understood.

"You understand," he said, "that she could not consent to see you before you knew just how weak she thought she had been." The judge stiffened to defiance in making this humiliation. "I don't consider, myself, that she was weak at all."

"Of course not!" Breckon beamed back at him.

"I consider that throughout she acted with the greatest - greatest - And that in that affair, when he behaved with that - that outrageous impudence, it was because she had misled the scoundrel by her kindness, her forbearance, her wish not to do him the least shadow of injustice, but to give him every chance of proving himself worthy of her tolerance; and -"

The judge choked, and Breckon eagerly asked, "And shall I - may I see her now?"

"Why - yes," the judge faltered. "If you're sure -"

"What about?" Breckon demanded.

"I don't know whether she will believe that I have told you."

"I will try to convince her. Where shall I see her?"

"I will go and tell her you are here. I will bring her -"

Kenton passed into the adjoining room, where his wife laid hold of him, almost violently. "You did it beautifully, Rufus," she huskily whispered, "and I was so afraid you would spoil everything. Oh, how manly you were, and how perfect he was!

William Dean Howells

But now it's my turn, and I will go and bring Ellen - You will let me, won't you?"

"You may do anything you please, Sarah. I don't want to have any more of this," said the judge from the chair he had dropped into.

"Well, then, I will bring her at once," said Mrs. Kenton, staying only in her gladness to kiss him on his gray head; he received her embrace with a superficial sultriness which did not deceive her.

Ellen came back without her mother, and as soon as she entered the room, and Breckon realized that she had come alone, he ran towards her as if to take her in his arms. But she put up her hand with extended fingers, and held him lightly off.

"Did poppa tell you?" she asked, with a certain defiance. She held her head up fiercely, and spoke steadily, but he could see the pulse beating in her pretty neck.

"Yes, he told me -"

"And - well?"

"Oh, I love you, Ellen -"

"That isn't it. Did you care?"

Breckon had an inspiration, an inspiration from the truth that dwelt at the bottom of his soul and had never yet failed to save him. He let his arms fall and answered, desperately: "Yes, I did. I wished it hadn't happened." He saw the pulse in her neck cease to beat, and he swiftly added, "But I know that it happened just because you were yourself, and were so -"

"If you had said you didn't care," she breathlessly whispered, "I would never have spoken to you." He felt a conditional tremor creeping into the fingers which had been so rigid against his breast. "I don't see how I lived through it! Do you think you can?"

"I think so," he returned, with a faint, far suggestion of levity that brought from her an imperative, imploring -

"Don't!"

Then he added, solemnly, "It had no more to do with you, Ellen, than an offence from some hateful animal -"

"Oh, how good you are!" The fingers folded themselves, and her arms weakened so that there was nothing to keep him from drawing her to him. "What - what are you doing?" she asked, with her face smothered against his.

"Oh, Ell-en, Ellen, Ellen! Oh, my love, my dearest, my best!"

"But I have been such a fool!" she protested, imagining that she was going to push him from her, but losing herself in him more and more.

"Yes, yes, darling! I know it. That's why I love you so!"

XXVI

"There is just one thing," said the judge, as he wound up his watch that night, "that makes me a little uneasy still."

Mrs. Kenton, already in her bed turned her face upon him with a despairing "Tchk! Dear! What is it? I thought we had talked over everything."

"We haven't got Lottie's consent yet."

"Well, I think I see myself asking Lottie!" Mrs. Kenton began, before she realized her husband's irony. She added, "How could you give me such a start?"

"Well, Lottie has bossed us so long that I couldn't help mentioning it," said the judge.

It was a lame excuse, and in its most potential implication his suggestion proved without reason. If Lottie never gave her explicit approval to Ellen's engagement, she never openly opposed it. She treated it, rather, with something like silent contempt, as a childish weakness on Ellen's part which was beneath her serious consideration. Towards Breckon, her behavior hardly changed in the severity which she had assumed from the moment she first ceased to have any use for him. "I suppose I will have to kiss him," she said, gloomily, when her mother told her that he was to be her brother, and she performed the rite with as much coldness as was ever put in that form of affectionate welcome. It is doubtful if Breckon perfectly realized its coldness; he never knew how much he enraged her by acting as if she were a little girl, and saying lightly, almost trivially, "I'm so glad you're going to be a sister to me."

With Ellen, Lottie now considered herself quits, and from the first hour of Ellen's happiness she threw off all the care with all the apparent kindness which she had used towards her when she was a morbid invalid. Here again, if Lottie had minded such a thing, she might have been as much vexed by Ellen's attitude as by Breckon's. Ellen never once noticed the withdrawal of her anxious oversight, or seemed in the least to miss it. As much as her meek nature would allow, she arrogated to herself the privileges and prerogatives of an elder sister, and if it had been possible to make Lottie ever feel like a chit, there were moments when Ellen's behavior would have made her feel like a chit. It was not till after their return to Tuskingum that Lottie took her true place in relation to the affair, and in the preparations for the wedding, which she appointed to be in the First Universalist Church, overruling both her mother's and sister's preferences for a home wedding, that Lottie rose in due authority. Mrs. Kenton had not ceased to feel quelled whenever her younger daughter called her mother instead of momma, and Ellen seemed not really to care. She submitted the matter to Breckon, who said, "Oh yes, if Lottie wishes," and he laughed when Ellen confessed, "Well, I said we would."

With the lifting of his great anxiety, he had got back to that lightness which was most like him, and he could not always conceal from Lottie herself that he regarded her as a joke. She did not mind it, she said, from such a mere sop as, in the vast content of his love, he was.

This was some months after Lottie had got at Scheveningen from Mr. Plumpton that letter which decided her that she had no use for him. There came the same day, and by the same post with it, a letter from one of her young men in Tuskingum, who had faithfully written to her all the winter before, and had not intermitted his letters after she went abroad. To Kenton he had always seemed too wise if not too good for Lottie, but Mrs. Kenton, who had her own doubts of Lottie, would not allow this when it came to the question, and said, woundedly, that she did not see why Lottie was not fully his equal in every way.

"Well," the judge suggested, "she isn't the first young lawyer at the Tuskingum bar."

"Well, I wouldn't wish her to be," said Mrs. Kenton, who did not often make jokes.

"Well, I don't know that I would," her husband assented, and he added, "Pretty good, Sarah."

"Lottie," her mother summed up, "is practical, and she is very neat. She won't let Mr. Elroy go around looking so slovenly. I hope she will make him have his hair cut, and not look as if it were bitten off. And I don't believe he's had his boots blacked since -"

"He was born," the judge proposed, and she assented.

"Yes. She is very saving, and he is wasteful. It will be a very good match. You can let them build on the other corner of the lot, if Ellen is going to be in New York. I would miss Lottie more than Ellen about the housekeeping, though the dear knows I will miss them both badly enough."

"Well, you can break off their engagements," said the judge.

As yet, and until Ellen was off her hands, Lottie would not allow Mr. Elroy to consider himself engaged to her. His conditional devotion did not debar him from a lover's rights, and, until Breckon came on from New York to be married, there was much more courtship of Lottie than of Ellen in the house. But Lottie saved herself in the form if not the fact, and as far as verbal terms were concerned, she was justified by them in declaring that she would not have another sop hanging round.

It was Boyne, and Boyne alone, who had any misgivings in regard to Ellen's engagement, and these were of a nature so recondite that when he came to impart them to his mother, before they left Scheveningen, and while there was yet time for that conclusion which his father suggested to Mrs. Kenton too late, Boyne had an almost hopeless difficulty in stating them. His approaches, even, were so mystical that his mother was forced to bring him to book sharply.

"Boyne, if you don't tell me right off just what you mean, I don't know what I will do to you! What are you driving at, for pity's sake? Are you saying that she oughtn't to be engaged to Mr. Breckon?"

"No, I'm not saying that, momma," said Boyne, in a distress that caused his mother to take a reef in her impatience.

"Well, what are you saying, then?"

"Why, you know how Ellen is, momma. You know how conscientious and - and - sensitive. Or, I don't mean sensitive, exactly."

"Well?"

"Well, I don't think she ought to be engaged to Mr. Breckon out of - gratitude."

"Gratitude?"

"Yes. I just know that she thinks - or it would be just like her - that he saved me that day. But he only met me about a second before we came to her and poppa, and the officers were taking me right along towards them." Mrs. Kenton held herself stormily in, and he continued: "I know that he translated for us before the magistrate, but the magistrate could speak a little

English, and when he saw poppa he saw that it was all right, anyway. I don't want to say anything against Mr. Breckon, and I think he behaved as well any one could; but if Ellen is going to marry him out of gratitude for saving me -"

Mrs. Kenton could hold in no longer. "And is this what you've been bothering the life half out of me for, for the last hour?"

"Well, I thought you ought to look at it in that light, momma."

"Well, Boyne," said his mother, "sometimes I think you're almost a fool!" and she turned her back upon her son and left him.

Boyne's place in the Kenton family, for which he continued to have the highest regard, became a little less difficult, a little less incompatible with his self-respect as time went on. His spirit, which had lagged a little after his body in stature, began, as his father said, to catch up. He no longer nourished it so exclusively upon heroical romance as he had during the past year, and after his return to Tuskingum he went into his brother Richard's once, and manifested a certain curiosity in the study of the law. He read Blackstone, and could give a fair account of his impressions of English law to his father. He had quite outlived the period of entomological research, and he presented his collections of insects (somewhat moth-eaten) to his nephew, on whom he also bestowed his postage-stamp album; Mary Kenton accepted them in trust, the nephew being of yet too tender years for their care. In the preoccupations of his immediate family with Ellen's engagement, Boyne became rather close friends with his sister-in-law, and there were times when he was tempted to submit to her judgment the question whether the young Queen of Holland did not really beckon to him that day. But pending the hour when he foresaw that Lottie should come out with the whole story, in some instant of excitement, Boyne had not quite the heart to speak of his experience. It assumed more and more respectability with him, and lost that squalor which had once put him to shame while it was yet new. He thought that Mary might be reasoned into regarding him as the hero of an adventure, but he is still hesitating whether to confide in her. In the meantime she knows all about it. Mary and Richard both approved of Ellen's choice, though they are somewhat puzzled to make out just what Mr. Breckon's religion is, and what his relations to his charge in New York may be. These do not seem to them quite pastoral, and he himself shares their uncertainty. But since his flock does not include Mrs. Rasmith and her daughter, he is content to let the question remain in abeyance. The Rasmiths are settled in Rome with an apparent permanency which they have not known elsewhere for a long time, and they have both joined in the friendliest kind of letter on his marriage to their former pastor, if that was what Breckon was. They have professed to know from the first that he was in love with Ellen, and that he is in love with her now is the strong present belief of his flock, if they are a flock, and if they may be said to have anything so positive as a belief in regard to anything.

Judge Kenton has given the Elroys the other corner of the lot, and has supplied them the means of building on it. Mary and Lottie run diagonally into the home-house every day, and nothing keeps either from coming into authority over the old people except the fear of each other in which they stand. The Kentons no longer make any summer journeys, but in the winter they take Boyne and go to see Ellen in New York. They do not stay so long as Mrs. Kenton would like. As soon as they have fairly seen the Breckons, and have settled comfortably down in their pleasant house on West Seventy-fourth Street, she detects him in a secret habit of sighing, which she recognizes as the worst symptom of homesickness, and then she confides to Ellen that she supposes Mr. Kenton will make her go home with him before long. Ellen knows it is useless to interfere. She even encourages her father's longings, so far as indulging his clandestine visits to the seedsman's, and she goes with him to pick up second-hand books about Ohio in the War at the dealers', who remember the judge very flatteringly.

As February draws on towards March it becomes impossible to detain Kenton. His wife and son return with him to Tuskingum, where Lottie has seen to the kindling of a good fire in the furnace against their arrival, and has nearly come to blows with Mary about provisioning them for the first dinner. Then Mrs. Kenton owns, with a comfort which she will not let her husband see, that there is no place like home, and they take up their life in the place where they have been so happy and so unhappy. He reads to her a good deal at night, and they play a game of checkers usually before they go to bed; she still cheats without scruple, for, as she justly says, he knows very well that she cannot bear to be beaten.

The colonel, as he is still invariably known to his veterans, works pretty faithfully at the regimental autobiography, and drives round the country, picking up material among them, in a buggy plastered with mud. He has imagined, since his last visit to Breckon, who dictates his sermons, if they are sermons, taking a stenographer with him, and the young lady, who is in deadly terror of the colonel's driving, is of the greatest use to him, in the case of veterans who will not or cannot give down (as they say in their dairy-country parlance), and has already rescued many reminiscences from perishing in their faltering memories. She writes them out in the judge's library when the colonel gets home, and his wife sometimes surprises Mr. Kenton correcting them there at night after she supposes he has gone to bed.

Since it has all turned out for the best concerning Bittridge, she no longer has those pangs of self-reproach for Richard's treatment of him which she suffered while afraid that if the fact came to Ellen's knowledge it might make her refuse Breckon. She does not find her daughter's behavior in the matter so anomalous as it appears to the judge.

He is willing to account for it on the ground of that inconsistency which he has observed in all human behavior, but Mrs. Kenton is not inclined to admit that it is so very inconsistent. She contends that Ellen had simply lived through that hateful episode of her psychological history, as she was sure to do sooner or later and as she was destined to do as soon as some other person arrived to take her fancy.

If this is the crude, common-sense view of the matter, Ellen herself is able to offer no finer explanation, which shall at the same time be more thorough. She and her husband have not failed to talk the affair over, with that fulness of treatment which young married people give their past when they have nothing to conceal from each other. She has attempted to solve the mystery by blaming herself for a certain essential levity of nature which, under all her appearance of gravity, sympathized with levity in others, and, for what she knows to the contrary, with something ignoble and unworthy in them. Breckon, of course, does not admit this, but he has suggested that she was first attracted to him by a certain unseriousness which reminded her of Bittridge, in enabling him to take her seriousness lightly. This is the logical inference which he makes from her theory of herself, but she insists that it does not follow; and she contends that she was moved to love him by an instant sense of his goodness, which she never lost, and in which she was trying to equal herself with him by even the desperate measure of renouncing her happiness, if that should ever seem her duty, to his perfection. He says this is not very clear, though it is awfully gratifying, and he does not quite understand why Mrs. Bittridge's letter should have liberated Ellen from her fancied obligations to the past. Ellen can only say that it did so by making her so ashamed ever to have had anything to do with such people, and making her see how much she had tried her father and mother by her folly. This again Breckon contends is not clear, but he says we live in a universe of problems in which another, more or less, does not much matter. He is always expecting that some chance shall confront him with Bittridge, and that the man's presence will explain everything; for, like so many Ohio people who leave their native State, the Bittridges have come East instead of going West, in quitting the neighborhood of Tuskingum. He is settled with his idolized mother in New York, where he is obscurely attached to one of the newspapers. That he has as yet failed to rise from the ranks in the great army of assignment men may be because moral quality tells everywhere, and to be a clever blackguard is not so well as to be simply clever. If ever Breckon has met his alter ego, as he amuses himself in calling him, he has not known it, though Bittridge may have been wiser in the case of a man of Breckon's publicity, not to call it distinction. There was a time, immediately after the Breckons heard from Tuskingum that the Bittridges were in New York, when Ellen's husband consulted her as to what might be his duty towards her late suitor in the event which has not taken place, and when he suggested, not too seriously, that Richard's course might be the solution. To his suggestion Ellen answered: "Oh no, dear! That was wrong," and this remains also Richard's opinion.

Choose from Thousands of 1stWorldLibrary Classics By

A. M. Barnard
Ada Leverson
Adolphus William Ward
Aesop
Agatha Christie
Alexander Aaronsohn
Alexander Kielland
Alexandre Dumas
Alfred Gatty
Alfred Ollivant
Alice Duer Miller
Alice Turner Curtis
Alice Dunbar
Allen Chapman
Ambrose Bierce
Amelia E. Barr
Amory H. Bradford
Andrew Lang
Andrew McFarland Davis
Andy Adams
Anna Alice Chapin
Anna Sewell
Annie Besant
Annie Hamilton Donnell
Annie Payson Call
Annie Roe Carr
Annonaymous
Anton Chekhov
Arnold Bennett
Arthur Conan Doyle
Arthur M. Winfield
Arthur Ransome
Arthur Schnitzler
Atticus
B.H. Baden-Powell
B. M. Bower
B. C. Chatterjee
Baroness Emmuska Orczy
Baroness Orczy
Basil King
Bayard Taylor
Ben Macomber
Bertha Muzzy Bower
Bjornstjerne Bjornson
Booth Tarkington
Boyd Cable
Bram Stoker
C. Collodi
C. E. Orr

C. M. Ingleby
Carolyn Wells
Catherine Parr Traill
Charles A. Eastman
Charles Amory Beach
Charles Dickens
Charles Dudley Warner
Charles Farrar Browne
Charles Ives
Charles Kingsley
Charles Klein
Charles Hanson Towne
Charles Lathrop Pack
Charles Romyn Dake
Charles Whibley
Charles Willing Beale
Charlotte M. Braeme
Charlotte M. Yonge
Charlotte Perkins Stetson
Clair W. Hayes
Clarence Day Jr.
Clarence E. Mulford
Clemence Housman
Confucius
Coningsby Dawson
Cornelis DeWitt Wilcox
Cyril Burleigh
D. H. Lawrence
Daniel Defoe
David Garnett
Dinah Craik
Don Carlos Janes
Donald Keyhoe
Dorothy Kilner
Dougan Clark
Douglas Fairbanks
E. Nesbit
E.P.Roe
E. Phillips Oppenheim
Earl Barnes
Edgar Rice Burroughs
Edith Van Dyne
Edith Wharton
Edward Everett Hale
Edward J. O'Biren
Edward S. Ellis
Edwin L. Arnold
Eleanor Atkins
Eliot Gregory

Elizabeth Gaskell
Elizabeth McCracken
Elizabeth Von Arnim
Ellem Key
Emerson Hough
Emilie F. Carlen
Emily Dickinson
Enid Bagnold
Enilor Macartney Lane
Erasmus W. Jones
Ernie Howard Pie
Ethel May Dell
Ethel Turner
Ethel Watts Mumford
Eugenie Foa
Eugene Wood
Eustace Hale Ball
Evelyn Everett-green
Everard Cotes
F. H. Cheley
F. J. Cross
F. Marion Crawford
Federick Austin Ogg
Ferdinand Ossendowski
Francis Bacon
Francis Darwin
Frances Hodgson Burnett
Frances Parkinson Keyes
Frank Gee Patchin
Frank Harris
Frank Jewett Mather
Frank L. Packard
Frank V. Webster
Frederic Stewart Isham
Frederick Trevor Hill
Frederick Winslow Taylor
Friedrich Kerst
Friedrich Nietzsche
Fyodor Dostoyevsky
G.A. Henty
G.K. Chesterton
Gabrielle E. Jackson
Garrett P. Serviss
Gaston Leroux
George A. Warren
George Ade
Geroge Bernard Shaw
George Durston
George Ebers

George Eliot
George Gissing
George MacDonald
George Meredith
George Orwell
George Sylvester Viereck
George Tucker
George W. Cable
George Wharton James
Gertrude Atherton
Gordon Casserly
Grace E. King
Grace Gallatin
Grace Greenwood
Grant Allen
Guillermo A. Sherwell
Gulielma Zollinger
Gustav Flaubert
H. A. Cody
H. B. Irving
H.C. Bailey
H. G. Wells
H. H. Munro
H. Irving Hancock
H. Rider Haggard
H. W. C. Davis
Haldeman Julius
Hall Caine
Hamilton Wright Mabie
Hans Christian Andersen
Harold Avery
Harold McGrath
Harriet Beecher Stowe
Harry Castlemon
Harry Coghill
Harry Houidini
Hayden Carruth
Helent Hunt Jackson
Helen Nicolay
Hendrik Conscience
Hendy David Thoreau
Henri Barbusse
Henrik Ibsen
Henry Adams
Henry Ford
Henry Frost
Henry James
Henry Jones Ford
Henry Seton Merriman
Henry W Longfellow
Herbert A. Giles

Herbert Carter
Herbert N. Casson
Herman Hesse
Hildegard G. Frey
Homer
Honore De Balzac
Horace B. Day
Horace Walpole
Horatio Alger Jr.
Howard Pyle
Howard R. Garis
Hugh Lofting
Hugh Walpole
Humphry Ward
Ian Maclaren
Inez Haynes Gillmore
Irving Bacheller
Isabel Hornibrook
Israel Abrahams
Ivan Turgenev
J.G.Austin
J. Henri Fabre
J. M. Barrie
J. Macdonald Oxley
J. S. Fletcher
J. S. Knowles
J. Storer Clouston
Jack London
Jacob Abbott
James Allen
James Andrews
James Baldwin
James Branch Cabell
James DeMille
James Joyce
James Lane Allen
James Lane Allen
James Oliver Curwood
James Oppenheim
James Otis
James R. Driscoll
Jane Austen
Jane L. Stewart
Janet Aldridge
Jens Peter Jacobsen
Jerome K. Jerome
John Burroughs
John Cournos
John F. Kennedy
John Gay
John Glasworthy

John Habberton
John Joy Bell
John Kendrick Bangs
John Milton
John Philip Sousa
Jonas Lauritz Idemil Lie
Jonathan Swift
Joseph A. Altsheler
Joseph Carey
Joseph Conrad
Joseph E. Badger Jr
Joseph Hergesheimer
Joseph Jacobs
Jules Vernes
Julian Hawthrone
Julie A Lippmann
Justin Huntly McCarthy
Kakuzo Okakura
Kenneth Grahame
Kenneth McGaffey
Kate Langley Bosher
Kate Langley Bosher
Katherine Cecil Thurston
Katherine Stokes
L. A. Abbot
L. T. Meade
L. Frank Baum
Latta Griswold
Laura Dent Crane
Laura Lee Hope
Laurence Housman
Lawrence Beasley
Leo Tolstoy
Leonid Andreyev
Lewis Carroll
Lewis Sperry Chafer
Lilian Bell
Lloyd Osbourne
Louis Hughes
Louis Tracy
Louisa May Alcott
Lucy Fitch Perkins
Lucy Maud Montgomery
Luther Benson
Lydia Miller Middleton
Lyndon Orr
M. Corvus
M. H. Adams
Margaret E. Sangster
Margret Howth
Margaret Vandercook

Margret Penrose
Maria Edgeworth
Maria Thompson Daviess
Mariano Azuela
Marion Polk Angellotti
Mark Overton
Mark Twain
Mary Austin
Mary Catherine Crowley
Mary Cole
Mary Hastings Bradley
Mary Roberts Rinehart
Mary Rowlandson
M. Wollstonecraft Shelley
Maud Lindsay
Max Beerbohm
Myra Kelly
Nathaniel Hawthrone
Nicolo Machiavelli
O. F. Walton
Oscar Wilde
Owen Johnson
P.G. Wodehouse
Paul and Mabel Thorne
Paul G. Tomlinson
Paul Severing
Percy Brebner
Peter B. Kyne
Plato
R. Derby Holmes
R. L. Stevenson
R. S. Ball
Rabindranath Tagore
Rahul Alvares
Ralph Bonehill
Ralph Henry Barbour
Ralph Victor
Ralph Waldo Emmerson
Rene Descartes
Rex Beach

Rex E. Beach
Richard Harding Davis
Richard Jefferies
Richard Le Gallienne
Robert Barr
Robert Frost
Robert Gordon Anderson
Robert L. Drake
Robert Lansing
Robert Lynd
Robert Michael Ballantyne
Robert W. Chambers
Rosa Nouchette Carey
Rudyard Kipling
Samuel B. Allison
Samuel Hopkins Adams
Sarah Bernhardt
Sarah C. Hallowell
Selma Lagerlof
Sherwood Anderson
Sigmund Freud
Standish O'Grady
Stanley Weyman
Stella Benson
Stella M. Francis
Stephen Crane
Stewart Edward White
Stijn Streuvels
Swami Abhedananda
Swami Parmananda
T. S. Ackland
T. S. Arthur
The Princess Der Ling
Thomas A. Janvier
Thomas A Kempis
Thomas Anderton
Thomas Bailey Aldrich
Thomas Bulfinch
Thomas De Quincey
Thomas Dixon

Thomas H. Huxley
Thomas Hardy
Thomas More
Thornton W. Burgess
U. S. Grant
Valentine Williams
Various Authors
Vaughan Kester
Victor Appleton
Victoria Cross
Virginia Woolf
Wadsworth Camp
Walter Camp
Walter Scott
Washington Irving
Wilbur Lawton
Wilkie Collins
Willa Cather
Willard F. Baker
William Dean Howells
William le Queux
W. Makepeace Thackeray
William W. Walter
William Shakespeare
Winston Churchill
Yei Theodora Ozaki
Yogi Ramacharaka
Young E. Allison
Zane Grey